pressing the limits

vertex editions ≈ california

Pressing the Limits is the catalogue for the exhibition
of the same name shown at the following venues:
Contemporary Arts Center, Las Vegas, NV
Dec. 4, 2008 – Jan. 23, 2009.
Arvada Center for the Arts and Humanities, Arvada, CO
March 6 – April 6, 2009
Golden West Gallery of Art, Huntington Beach, CA
Mar. 15 – April 12, 2012.

Many thanks to Mark Diederichsen, co-curator, and to Beate Kirmse,
executive director of the CAC Las Vegas, for their vision, dedication, and hard
work in helping make these exhibitions a reality. Many thanks also to Collin
Parson and Chuck McCoy, for helping to bring *Pressing the Limits* to Colorado,
and Professor Darrell Ebert for bringing the exhibit to California.

Editor: Mark Diederichsen

ISBN 13: 978-0692418727

ISBN-10: 0692418725

i n t r o d u c t i o n

The artists invited for the "Pressing the Limits" exhibition at the Contemporary Arts Center, in Las Vegas, Nevada, are all extraordinary printmakers. The artwork of Mitchell S. Marti, Jennifer Lynch, Willis F. Lee, and Michael Costello may differ in imagery and technical approach, but each piece is an example of printmaking that goes well beyond anticipated limits, expanding the definition of what a fine art print can look like, and what it can be.

Co-curated by Mark Diederichsen and Michael Costello, "Pressing the Limits" was conceived of as a conceptual exhibition, whose title refers to both technical sophistication in printmaking and a fascination, shared by the artists, with subject matter that explores limits and edges. There are subtle edges where aboveground meets underground, where light reflects off the surface of water, where clouds meet sky, where water beads up on shattered glass, and where crude oil held in the earth meets that earth. These edges are where limits are defined; the sky ceases to be sky only when it becomes sea, or earth, or cloud. At what point does the light dancing on the surface of water become the water. What actually happens at that intersection?

These are some of the physical limits referenced in the artworks, but aesthetic limits are also explored. Technical maps of underground oil reserves are not initially generated to become beautiful artworks, but they do contain a precise elegance, and in Mitchell

Marti's hands they are co-opted and articulated in a beautiful way. Non-Euclidian geometric equations (fractals) are not usually considered landscapes, but when Jennifer Lynch uses them to create solar plates and prints them with viscosity techniques, they show a hidden side of nature. Willis F. Lee explores the edges of reality and illusion, using photography's great strength of representing reality, and twisting it, until we no longer know what has been constructed in the darkroom, and what is "real".

Part of the conceptual framework of "Pressing the Limits" is to expand a definition of fine art printmaking to include "imprinting". Imprinting is what happens when light leaves its energy pattern in a strip of film, when ferric chloride travels through a gelatin photogravure tissue and etches into a copper plate, and what also happens when the ink from a printing plate transfers to the paper in a printing press. This inclusion of "imprinting" as part of an expanding definition of printmaking, allows for photography, and digital imaging, to be rightfully recognized as part of the expanded printmaking family. It is a definition after the fact; the artists included in "Pressing the Limits" were already creating these prints, this conceptual framework was invented to describe what they are doing, and to help describe what these very diverse printmakers have in common.

Michael Costello

p r e s s i n g   t h e   l i m i t s

f o u r   c o n t e m p o r a r y
a m e r i c a n   p r i n t m a k e r s

or, "the Fable of the Photon"

A particle called light departs from a distant star. It travels leisurely for a thousand years, undulating in its waveform. It encounters no thing in the vacuum of space, and does not experience time passing until it suddenly slams into the fast moving water of a New Mexico stream. It bounces off the water, passes through refined glass, and is buried in the emulsion side of a strip of film. The photon dies as the film absorbs its energy, but its death leaves an impression. The photographer etches its memory in silver- and hangs the print on the wall of the Las Vegas CAC...

At the same time, in a studio in Taos, a printmaker rolls blended ink onto an etched solar plate. She carefully adjusts the colors, seeking the right combination of vibrations of light. When the plate is fully inked, and the colors are balanced, she places it on the press. The plate is covered with damp paper and it disappears from view. It travels through the press, driven by pressure, and the ink adhering to its surface leaves it for the receptive jungle of the fibers of the paper. When it emerges on the other side of the press, the plate is depleted, exhausted. The image carefully constructed on the plate's surface is gone- but an impression of it remains, buried in the fibers of the paper. This print also travels, and hangs on the wall of the Las Vegas CAC...

If this story is a fable, then the events described must contain a moral, a meaning beyond the simple telling. The photon has transformed into a phantom, a ghost, the image on the plate has ceased to exist. What meaning is conveyed by those impressions left behind? What do we see? What do we understand? A viewer in the art gallery decides one meaning, a personal one, relative to that viewer's experience – but the essential meaning, *das Ding an sich*, is that the action of imprinting, in itself, created the meaning. Before the imprinting the print did not exist, the meaning of the impression did not exist; afterwards it is there to be discovered.

I have been creating fine art prints in many forms, for many artists, for many years. I have always been struck and fascinated by that moment when the plate, covered and hidden by the paper, has gone through the press, but the paper has not yet been lifted from the plate. The artist stands by the press and stares expectantly at the blank back of the paper, everyone allowed to be in the studio is watching. The printer then pulls the paper up, and the print is revealed. The artist is relieved, satisfied and pleased (or disappointed, or angry). Either way, it is done, and it cannot be undone. The ink has left the plate and traveled into the paper. The plate has been depleted, used up, but its impression, reversed and imbedded into the paper, has now come into existence. A work of art has been created. If, however, a plate is prepared and inked, and for any reason not printed, there is a slight, but palpable, sense of loss in the studio – of a completion not arrived at, of an idea conceived of, but not born. We missed that feeling of energy and excitement, which is always released in that moment of imprinting. We miss that energy because it feeds us, and whenever we don't complete the action of printing the plate, we aren't being fed.

We never get to see the exact moment of creation, of imprinting, of transference. The photon that leaves its mark on a filmstrip is buried in its chemistry, and not in our eye. The ink that travels from plate to paper does so out of the range of our vision. We have to let it go. We try to get as close as we possibly can; we meticulously direct the material (photons or ink), and we can know a great deal about our chosen process, but we never can see it happen, or even pinpoint in our minds that precise instant when the impression takes place. This inability of perception, of precise definition, is a philosophical conundrum. It is an ancient one, and I won't be able to solve it here. I would like to speak of meaning, however, and how it functions in making prints.

Just before the point of penetration into the film, the photon from the star has already traveled a long distance, but because it has not physically interacted with any other particles, it has not left an impression. After it has exploded into the film, lost its form and left its impression, its story can be told. It is the photographer's job to tell that photon's story – gently transforming that impression in the film (now a chemical map) into a photographic print; one that we can see, and hang on the wall. We can look at the photograph and discern that it is starlight, or at least a cognate image of that starlight. It now has meaning for us; we look at it and our mind says "starlight". We remember what starlight looks like, and how it makes us feel.

This point is key: it is our memory of starlight that provides for us our understanding of it. If we had never before seen starlight, if we had no memory of it, we wouldn't be able to recognize it; its image would hold no meaning for us. When we see starlight (or any thing) for the first time, we begin to create a meaning for it, filing it away in our brains, along with attending emotions, sounds, and smells; it has left an impression.

It has left an impression: this description is not a metaphor; it is a precise expression of what has physically happened. A particle called light enters the eye, travels through the iris, and is imprinted on the rods and cones. This imprinting of the light particle creates an electro-chemical stimulus that travels to the brain. A chemically encoded signature is imprinted in the brain, this is called a memory, and recalling this memory is what creates a meaning.

In printmaking it is the same.

I have often been asked, "why make monotypes, why make prints at all, go through all these very technical and difficult steps when one can easily make a painting directly on the canvas or paper?" I have given many different answers to that question; that it is energizing and freeing to work in a collaboration with a master printer, that the results garnered in fine art printmaking cannot be achieved any other way, that there is a special luminescent quality to ink pressed into a beautiful paper, and all these answers are true. I always knew, however, that when I gave those answers, I wasn't quite telling the story whole.

The imprinted memory of the image prepared by the artist on the surface of the plate, also simply called *the print* (or monotype, or lithograph, or etching, or woodblock), holds a meaning greater than the meaning of the unprinted template. The print is more meaningful. How is this possible? Isn't the print a mere translation of the artist's intent, a generation removed from the direct hand? The answer is that the very action of imprinting has increased its meaning.

Just as a fresh experience of starlight, by the virtue of being imprinted, again, in our brains, creates a more full and meaningful knowledge of "starlight", the imprinting of an inked plate into paper creates a more full and meaningful knowledge of the image (idea) which was drawn upon it. The image printed has a built-in history. It was something else, became transformed, and is richer for the transformation.

Is the similarity of processes (between creating memories and creating fine art prints) merely a coincidence, not actually equivalence? Is the idea a just play of words, a wisp of cloud that disappears when you try to hold it in your mind? The answers to these questions are "perhaps", and "maybe"; but I have stood next to the press and experienced that particular moment of imprinting ten thousand times. I know in my bones that the finished print holds an expanded meaning, and if I haven't been able to convince the reader, then the fault is in the telling, and not in the reality of what I have tried to express.

Besides, this is a fable, and in fables all metaphors are true.

Michael Costello
Hand Graphics, Santa Fe, New Mexico, 2009

Willis F. Lee

Jennifer Lynch

Mitchell Marti

Michael Costello

Willis F. Lee

Willis F. Lee, a photographer/printmaker, produces exquisite copperplate photogravures, silver-prints, C-prints, digital prints, and directly exposed photograms of plants above and below the earth. His work can be humorous, or profound, and sometimes both. His prints are always beautifully conceived, and technically impeccable. Mr. Lee has his expansive photographic darkroom and photogravure studio at his home in Santa Fe, NM.

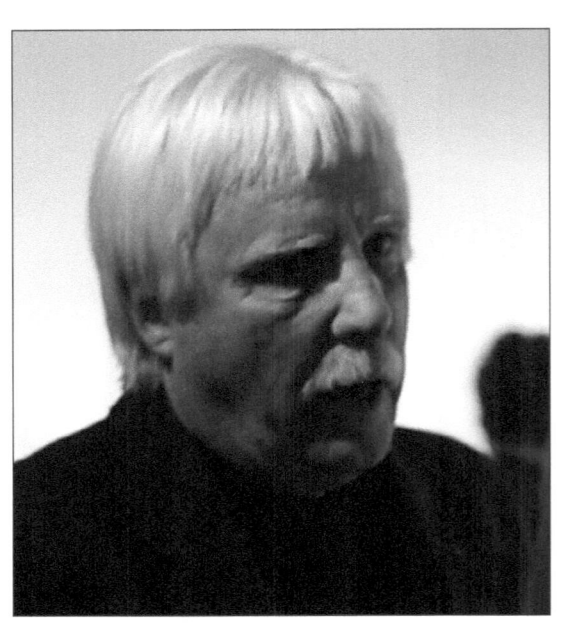

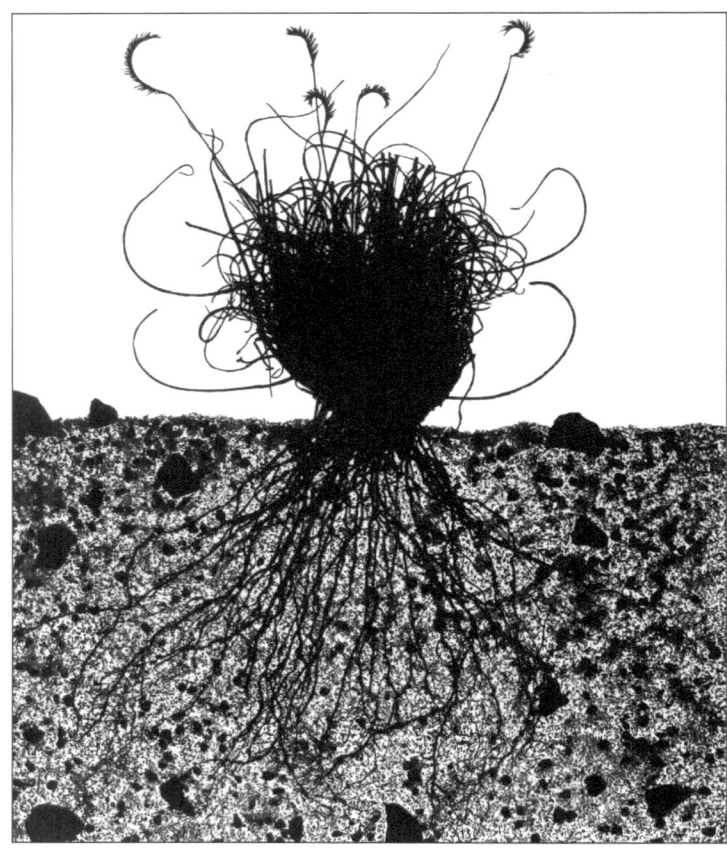

Subjacent I, *gelatin silver print, 21 ½ x 18 ⅞ inches*

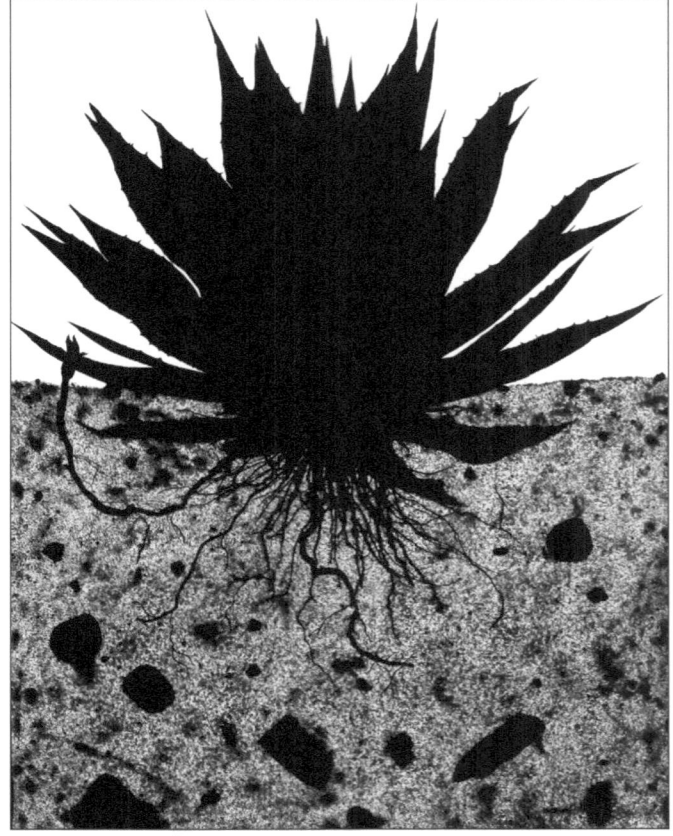

Subjacent II, *gelatin silver print, 21 ½ x 18 ⅞ inches*

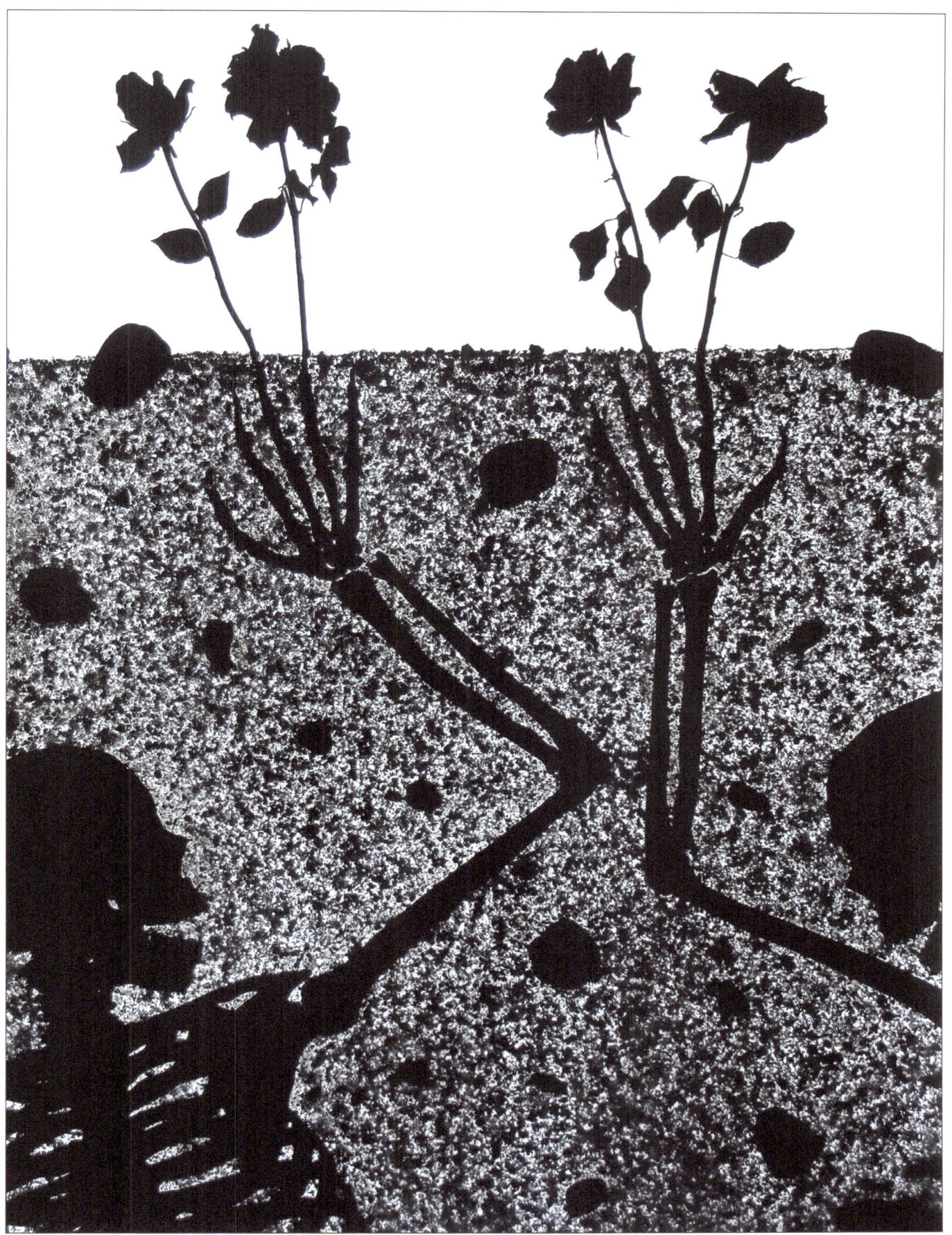

Subjacent X, *gelatin silver print, 51 ½ x 41 ⅛ inches*

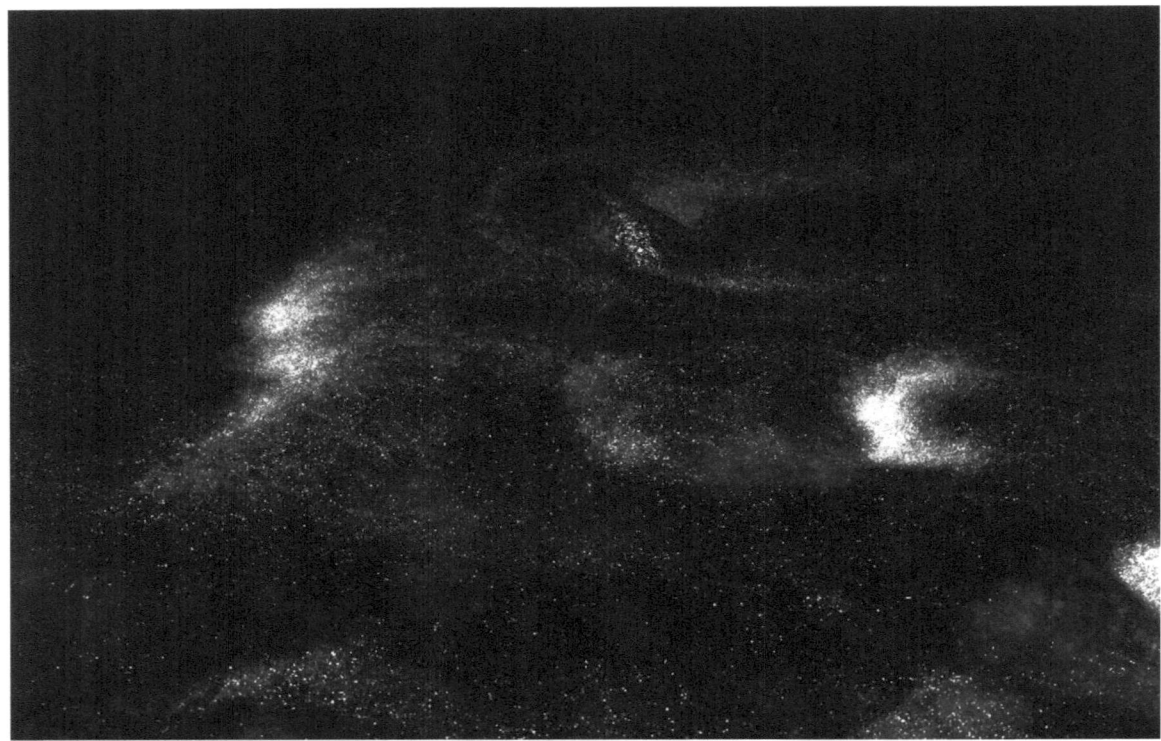

Pecos River at Night 3, *gelatin silver print, 27 ⅞ x 33 inches*

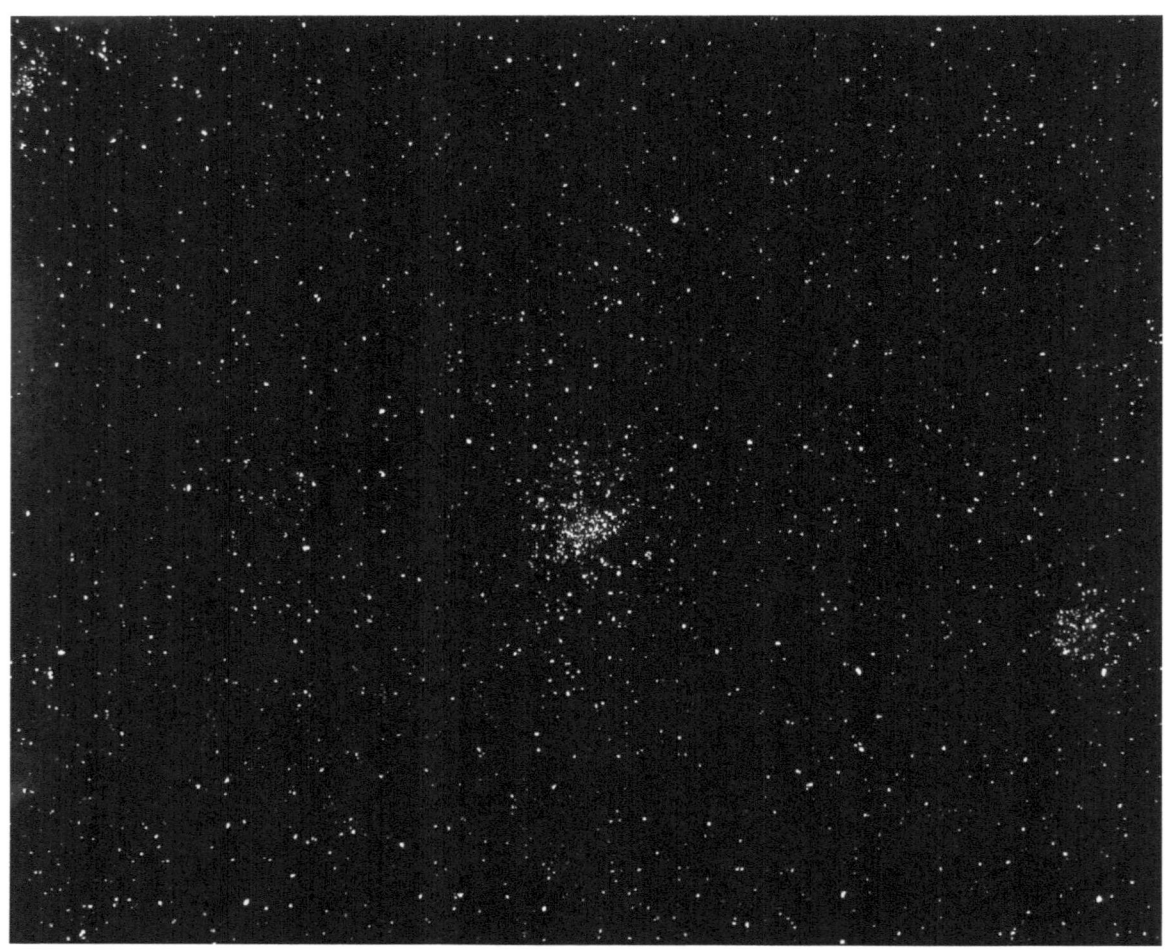

For Every Grain of Sand, *gelatin silver print, 27 ⅞ x 33 inches*

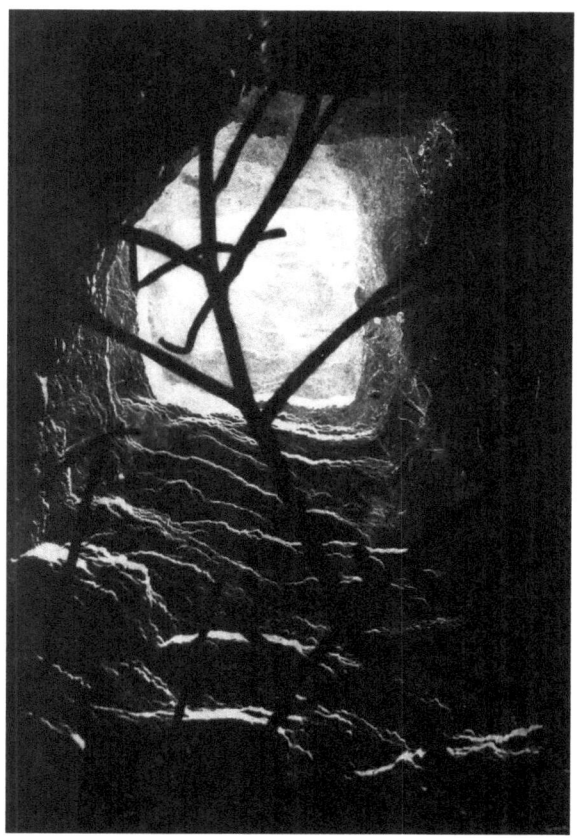

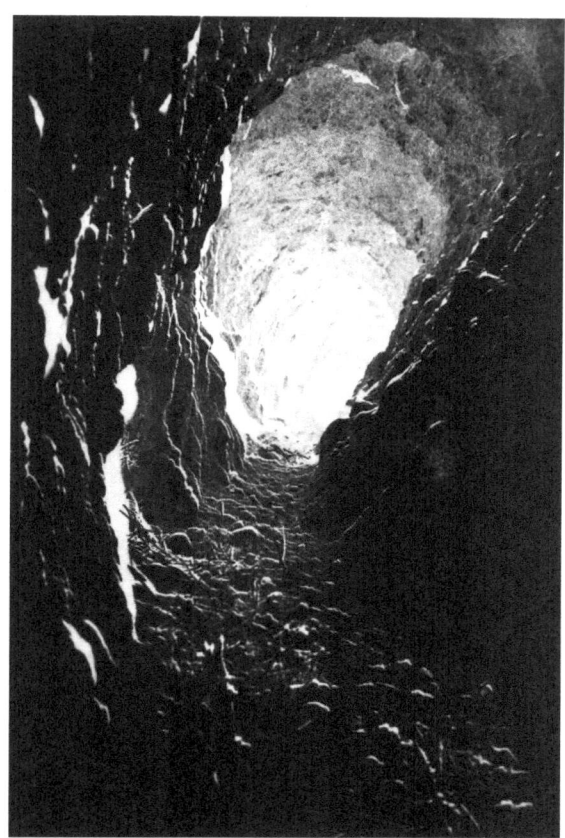

Coyote Caves IV, *copperplate gravure, 17 x 14 ³/₄ inches*　　Coyote Caves V, *copperplate gravure, 17 x 14 ³/₄ inches*

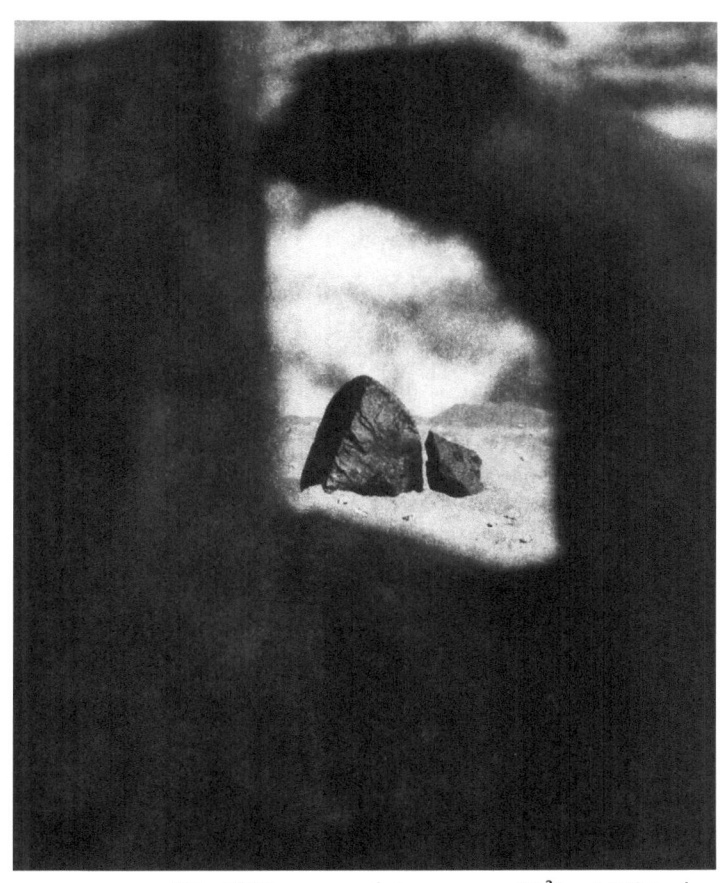

Site 1221, *copperplate gravure, 16 ³/₄ x 14 ⁷/₈ inches*

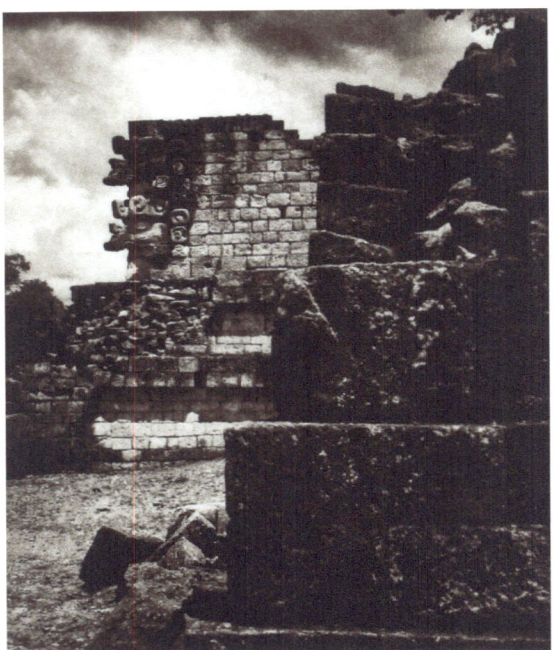

Copán: Plate V, *copperplate gravure, 20 ³/₄ x 16 ³/₄ inches*

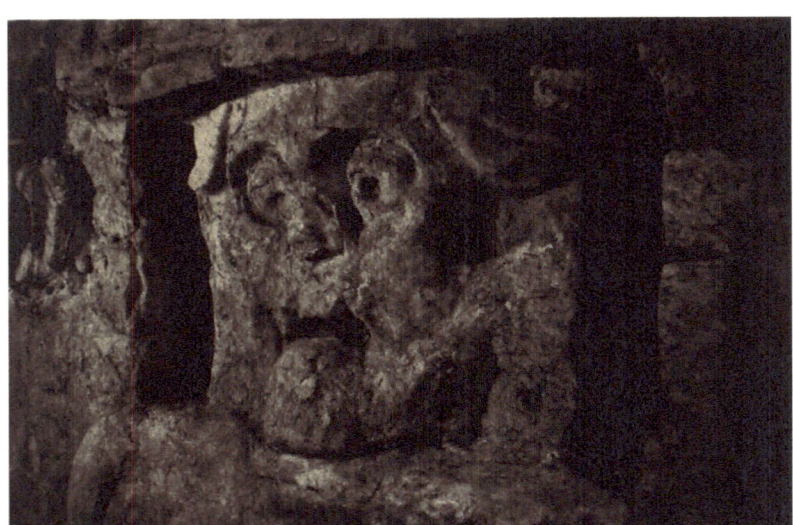

Copán: Plate XII, *copperplate gravure, 16 ³/₄ x 20 ³/₄ inches*

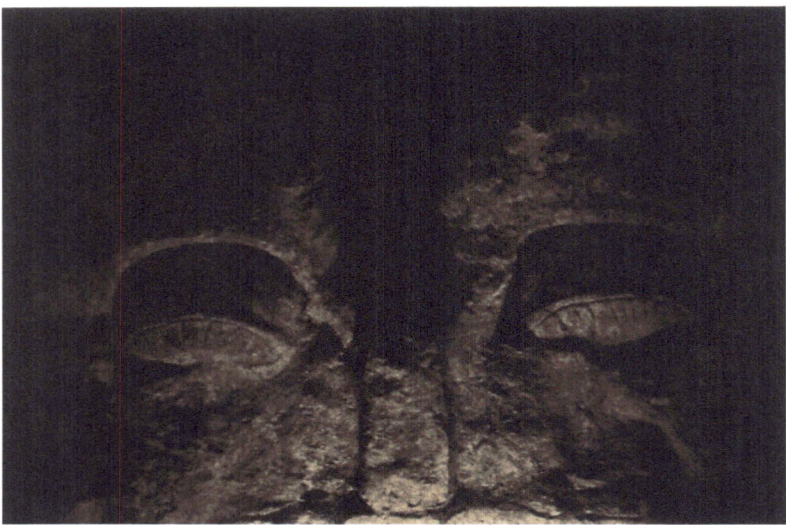

Copán: Plate III, *copperplate gravure, 16 ³/₄ x 20 ³/₄ inches*

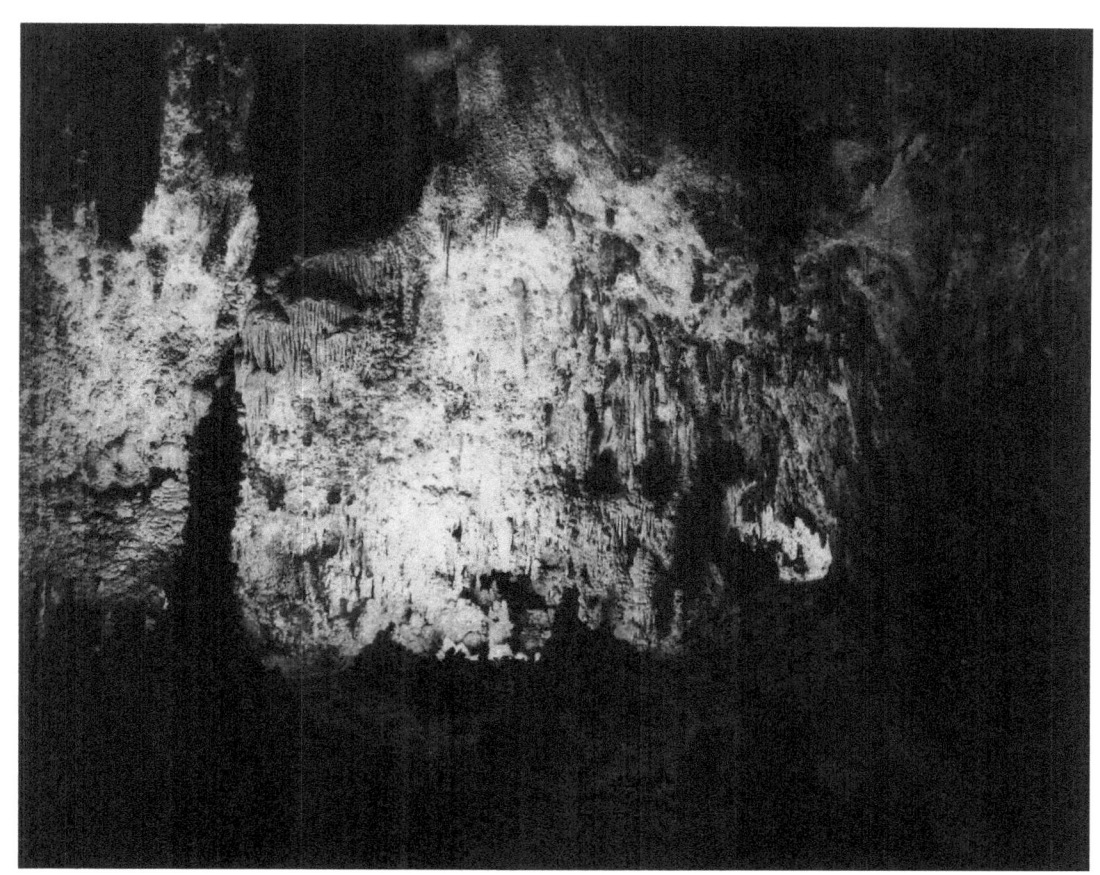

Allegory of the Cave: Plate I, *copperplate gravure, 19 ¹/₄ x 22 inches*

Allegory of the Cave: Plate II, *copperplate gravure, 22 x 19 ¹/₄ inches*

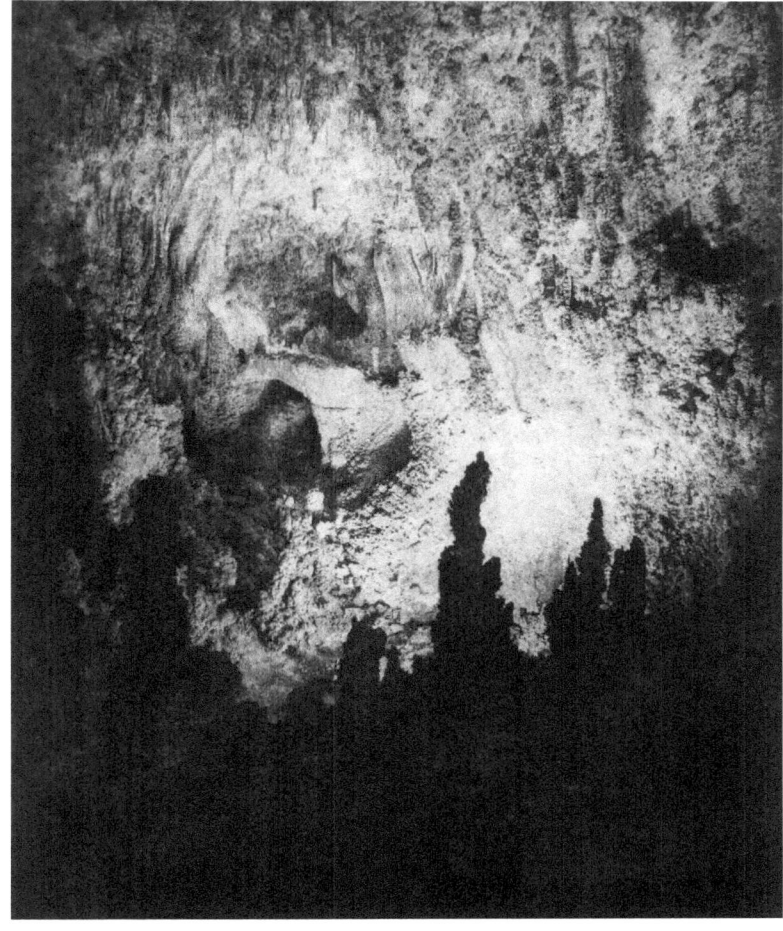

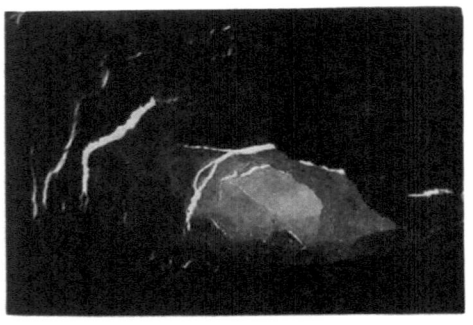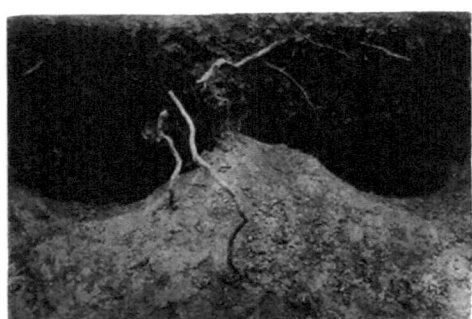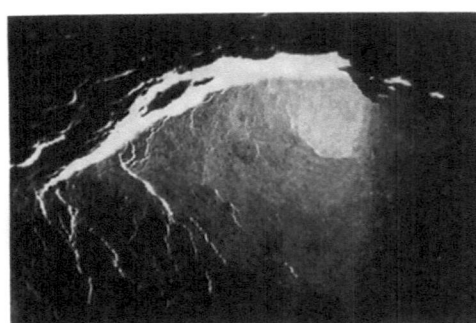

Coyote Caves, *copperplate gravure, 15 ⅝ x 31 ¼ inches*

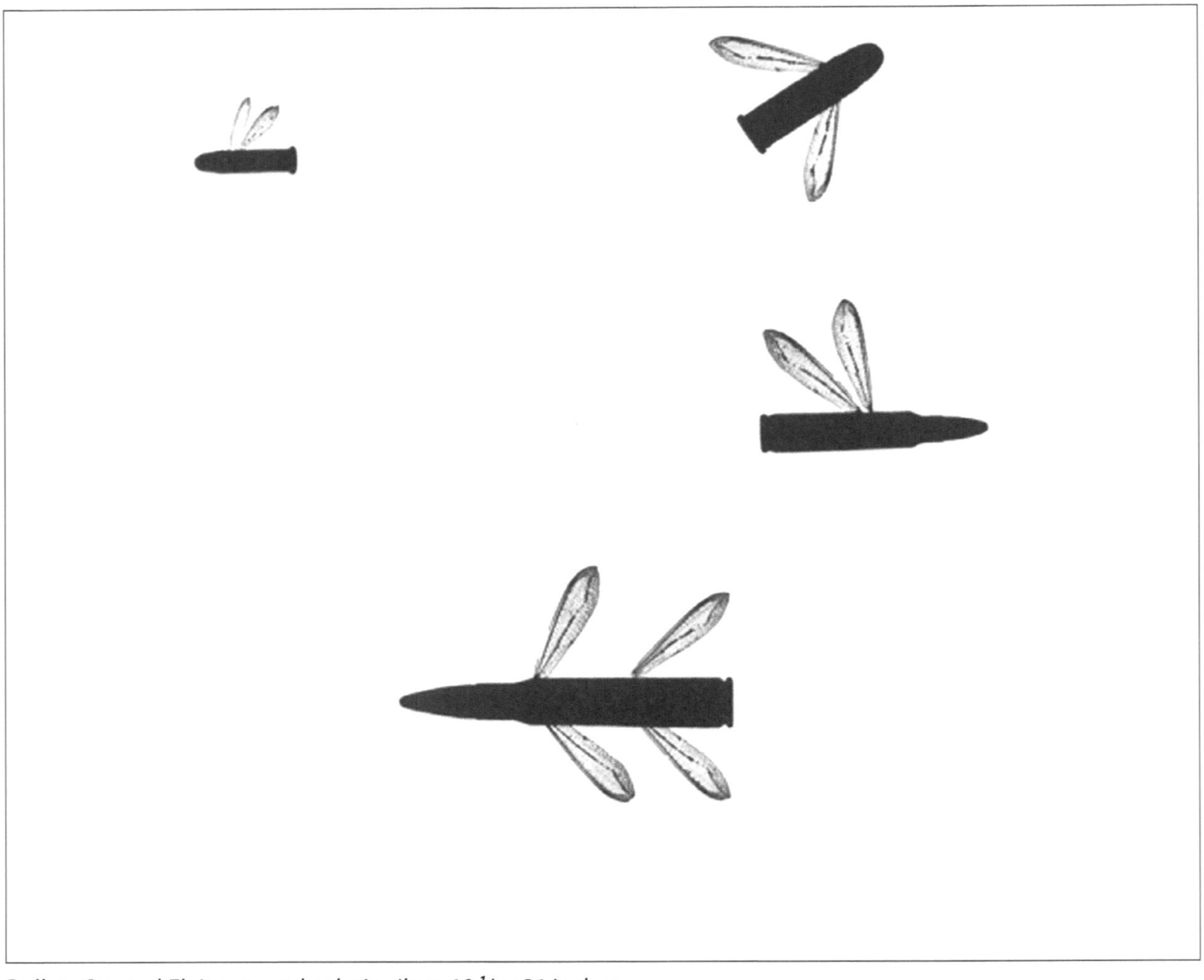

Bullets Started Flying, *toned gelatin silver, 19 ½ x 21 inches*

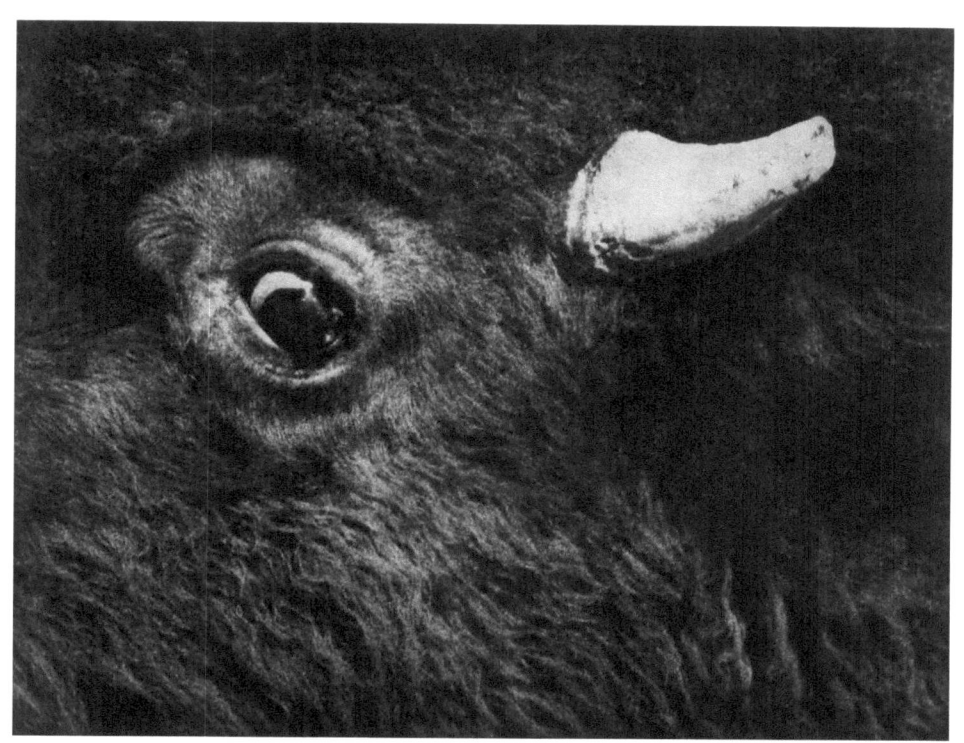

Fear, *copperplate gravure, 16 ¹/₄ x 23 inches*

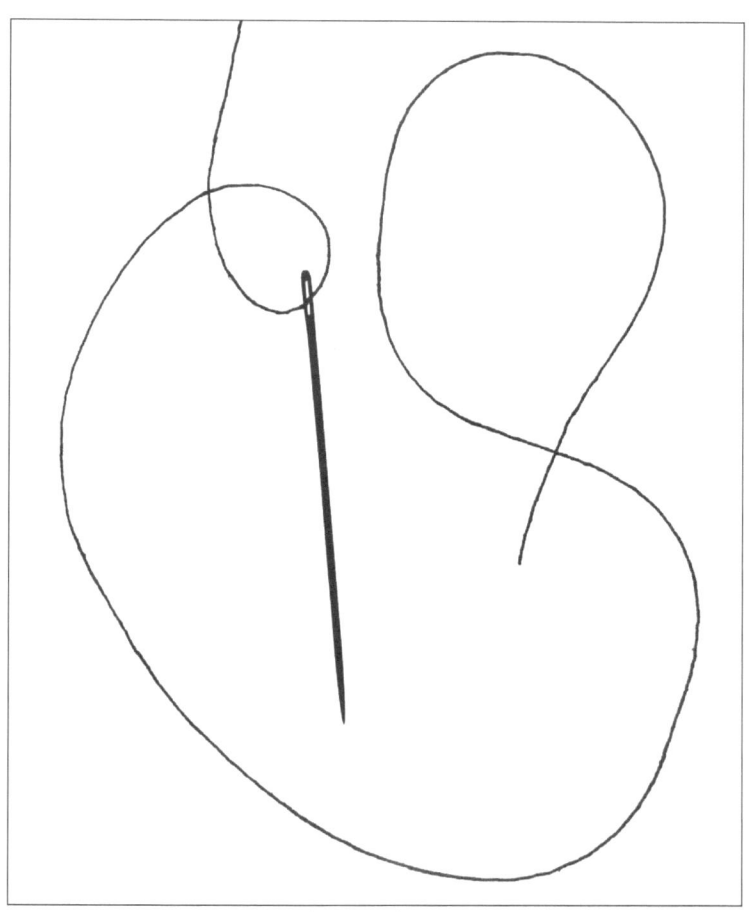

Needle and Thread, *gelatin silver print, 29 x 24*

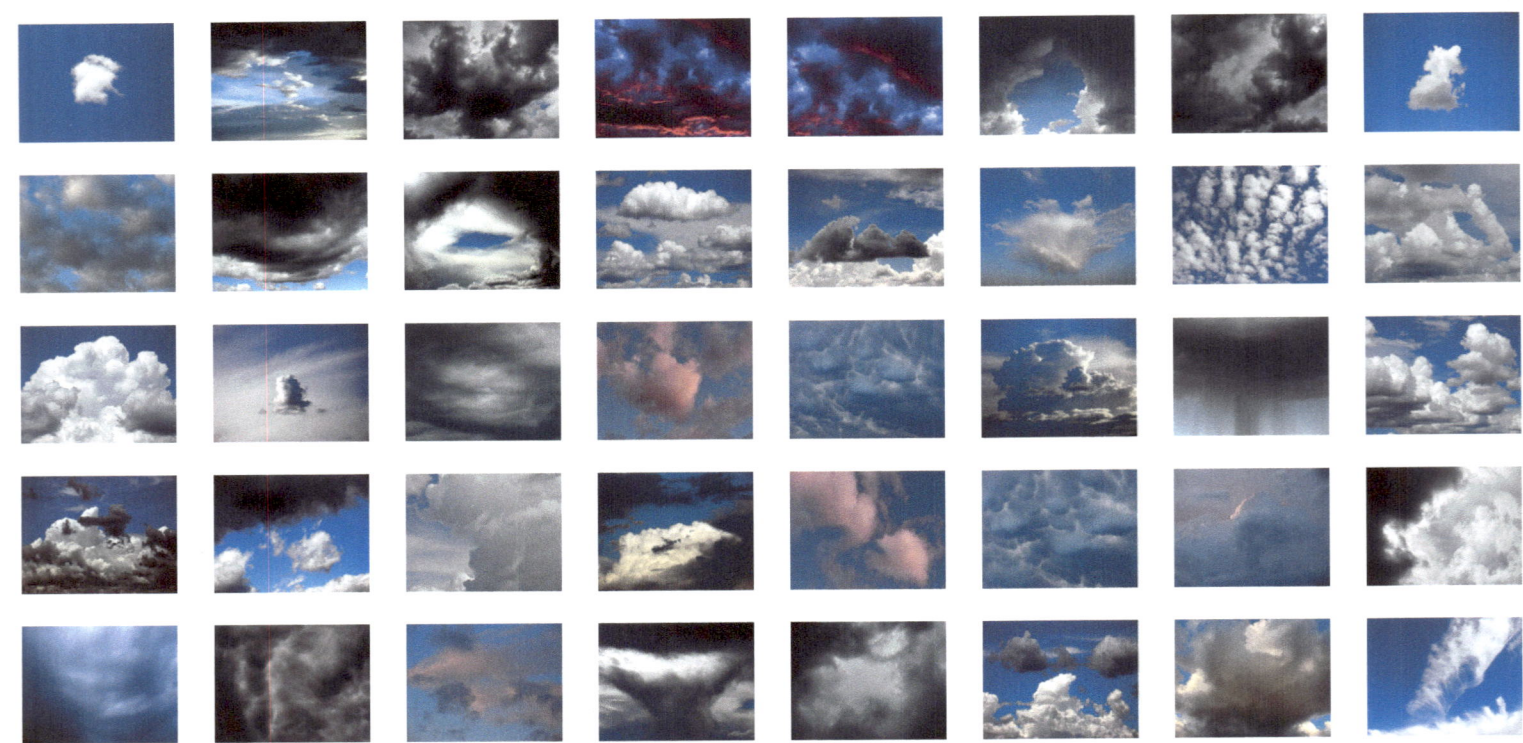

Ephemeral, *pigment prints, 49 ¹/₄ x 97 ¹/₄ inches*

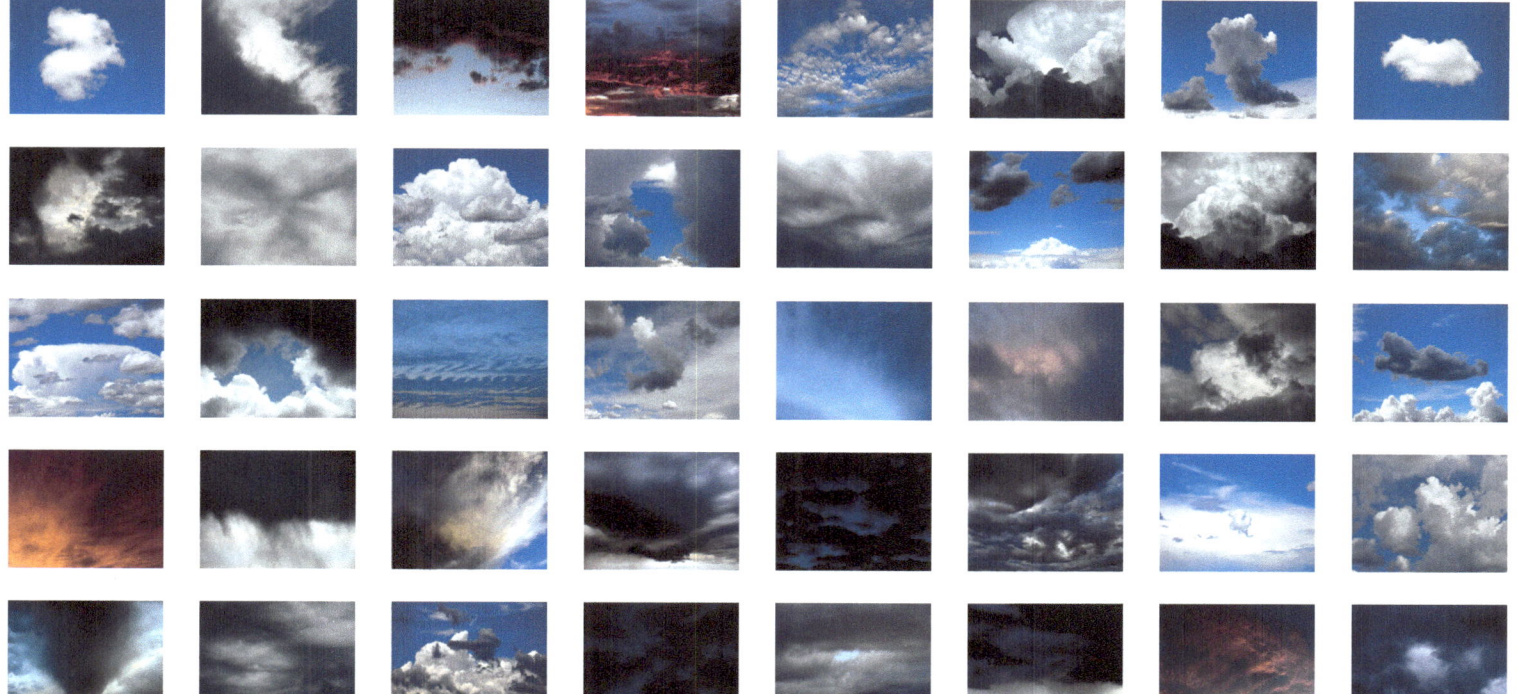

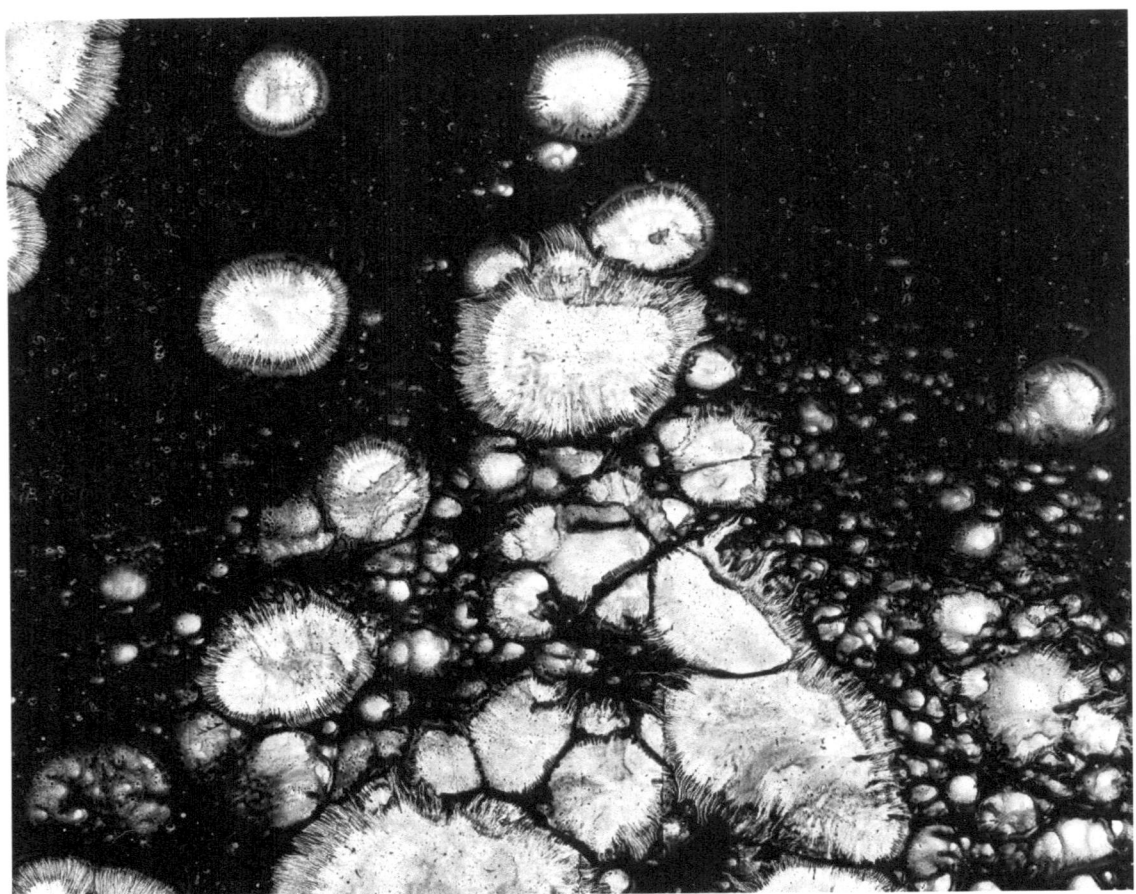

Pecos River Anomaly II, *pigment print, 31 x 36 inches*

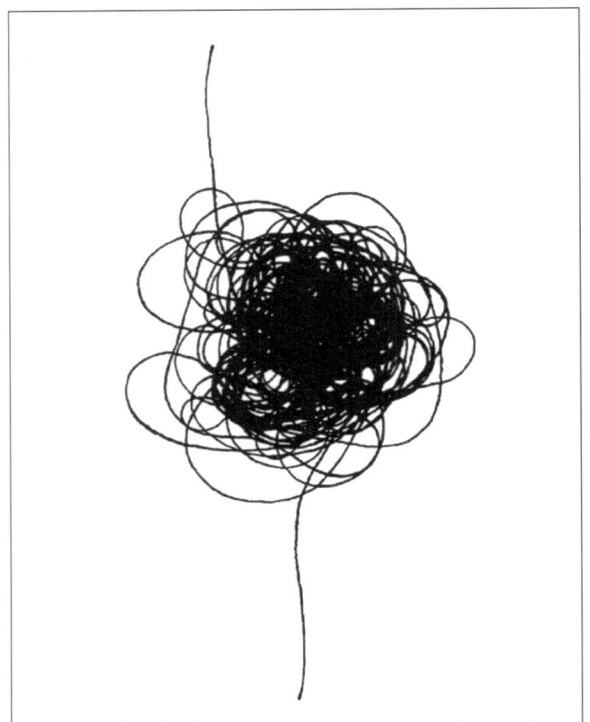

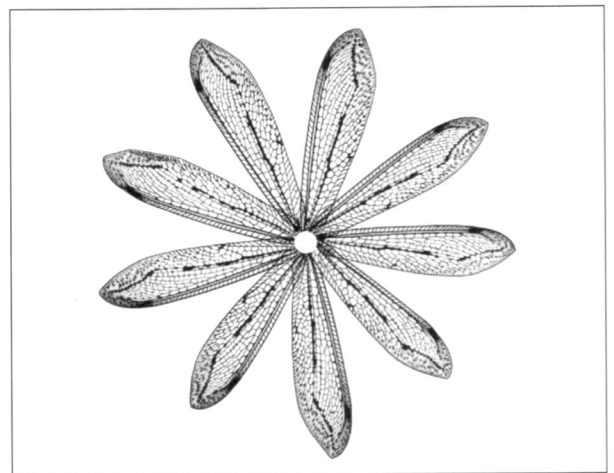

Wings, *toned gelatin silver, 25 x 25 ⁵/₈ inches*

Untitled (Ball of Thread), *toned gelatin silver, 29 ¹/₈ x 24 ¹/₂ inches*

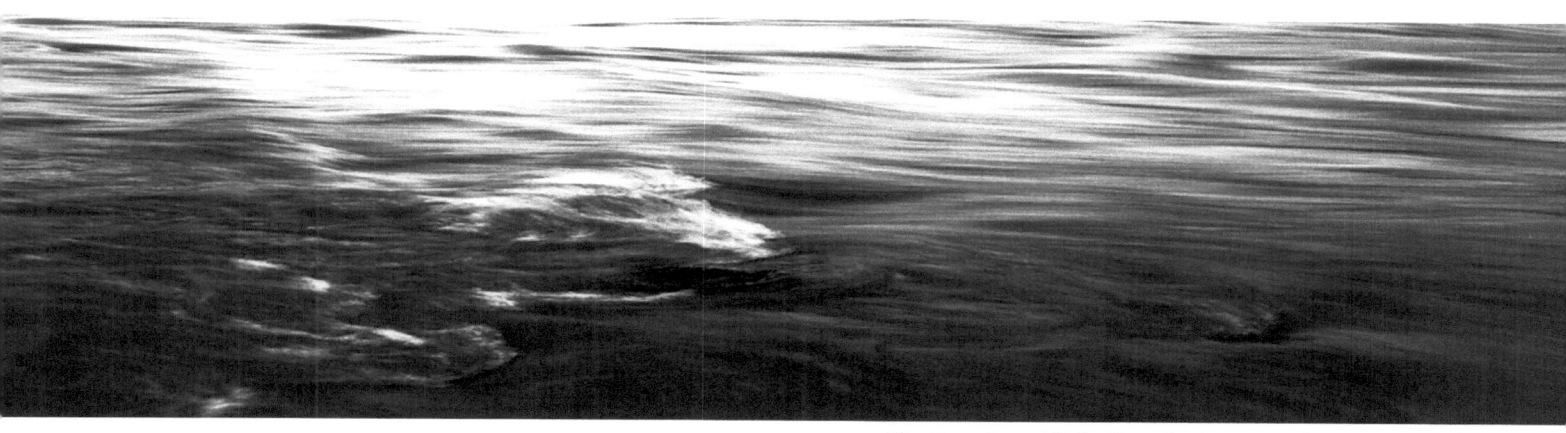

Rio Grande at Night Detail, *pigment print, 25 x 91 inches*

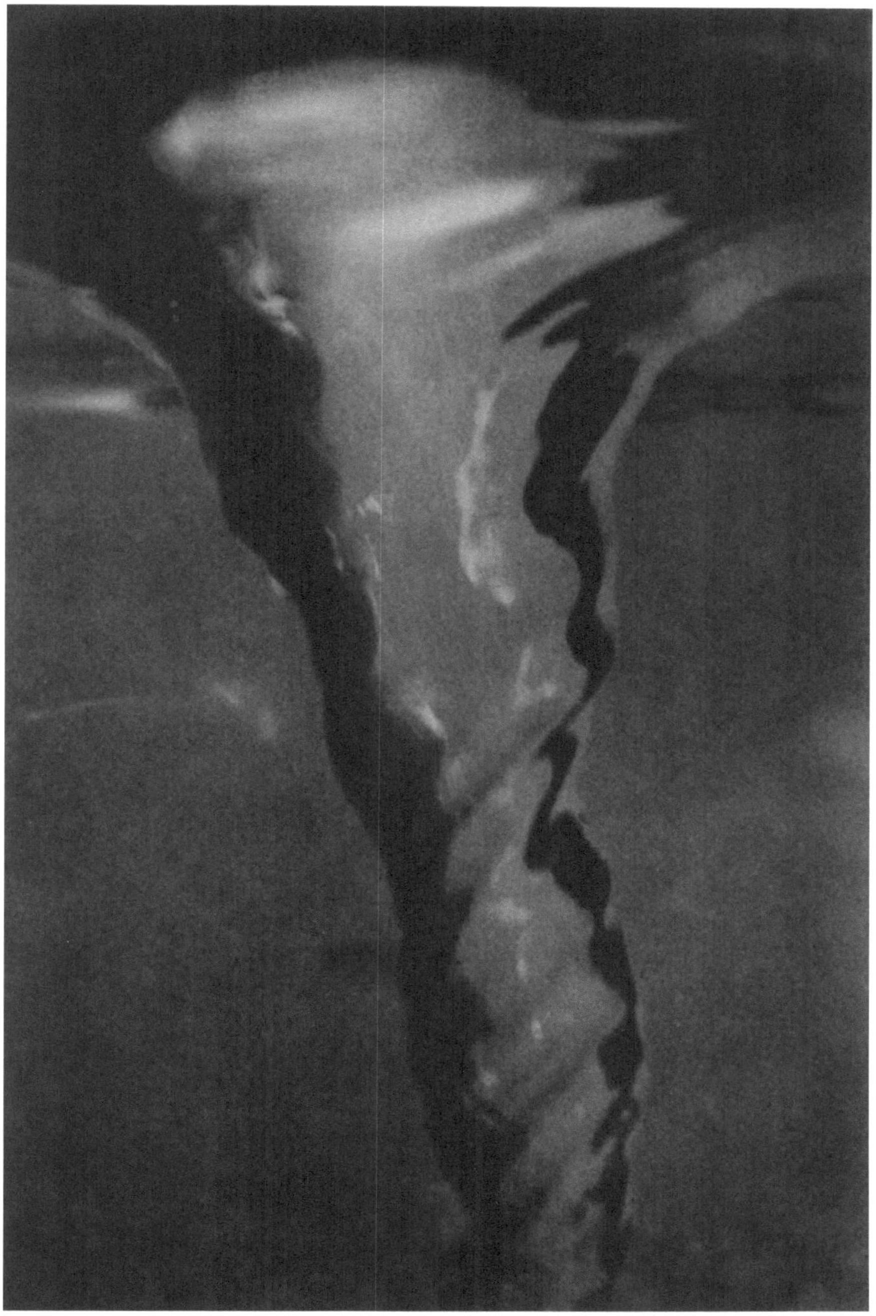

Vortex, *copperplate gravure, 16 ³⁄₄ x 14 ³⁄₄ inches*

Jennifer Lynch

Jennifer Lynch creating her artwork by pressing the limits of form and technical virtuosity. Her "Fractal" series explores a non-Euclidian geometry translated into solar-plate viscosity etchings. The results are edition prints of lively and lovely color; the forms generated from fractal equations suggest brilliant landscapes as seen from the sky. The CL (cosmic light) series explores the light and color that comes out of the darkness of space. The large photolithographs (L-series) depict the intersection of glass and water-drops, the limits of reflection and refraction. Ms. Lynch is the owner and master printer of LynchPin Press, a professional collaborative printmaking studio in Taos, NM.

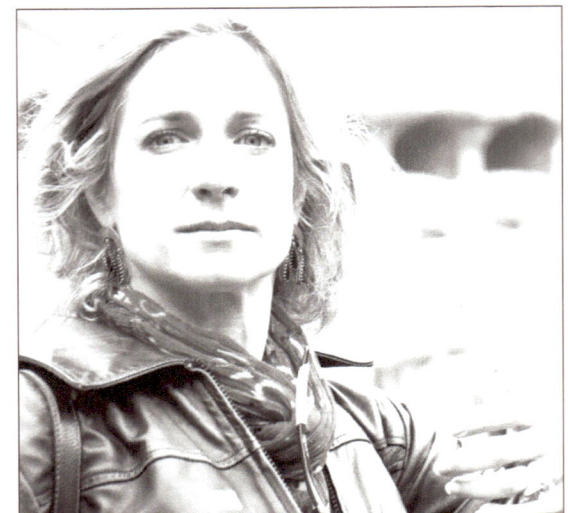

Photo: Marjorie Olson

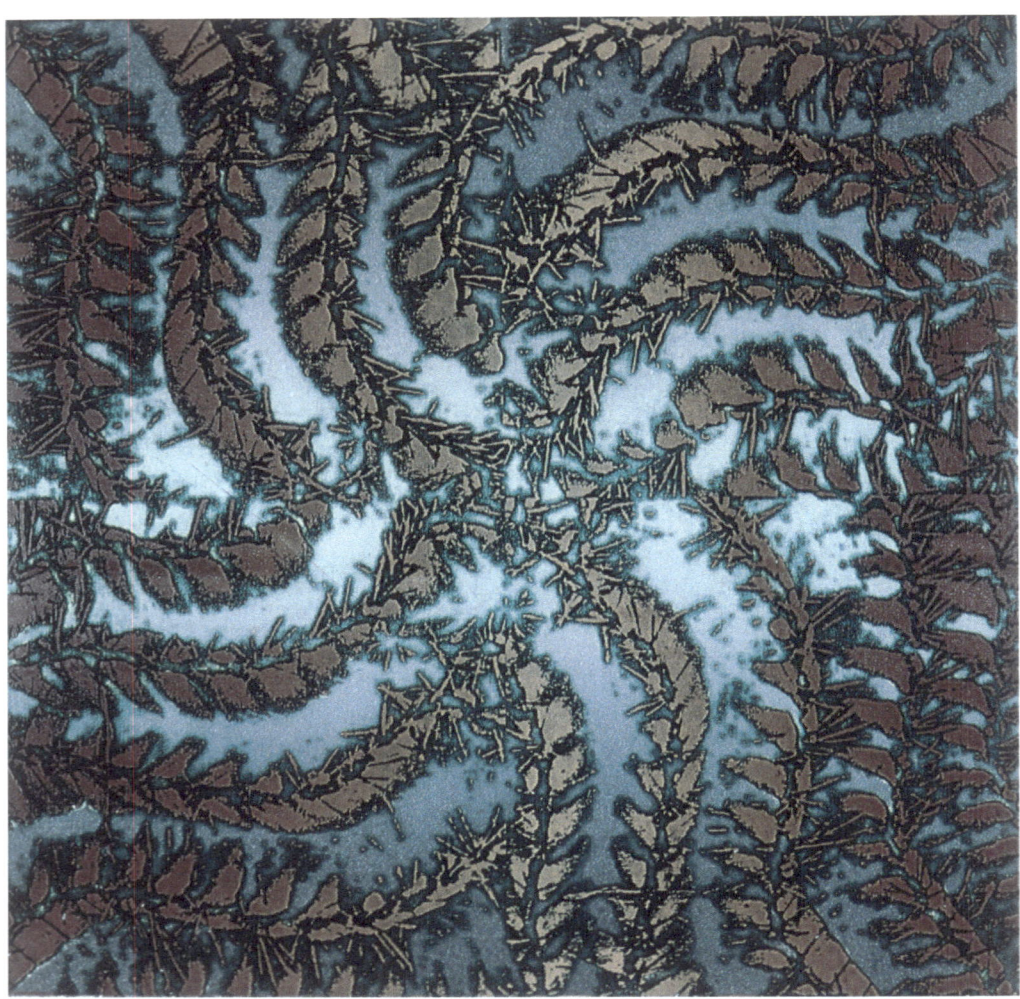

Fractal 13, *viscosity solarplate etching, 18 x 18 inches*

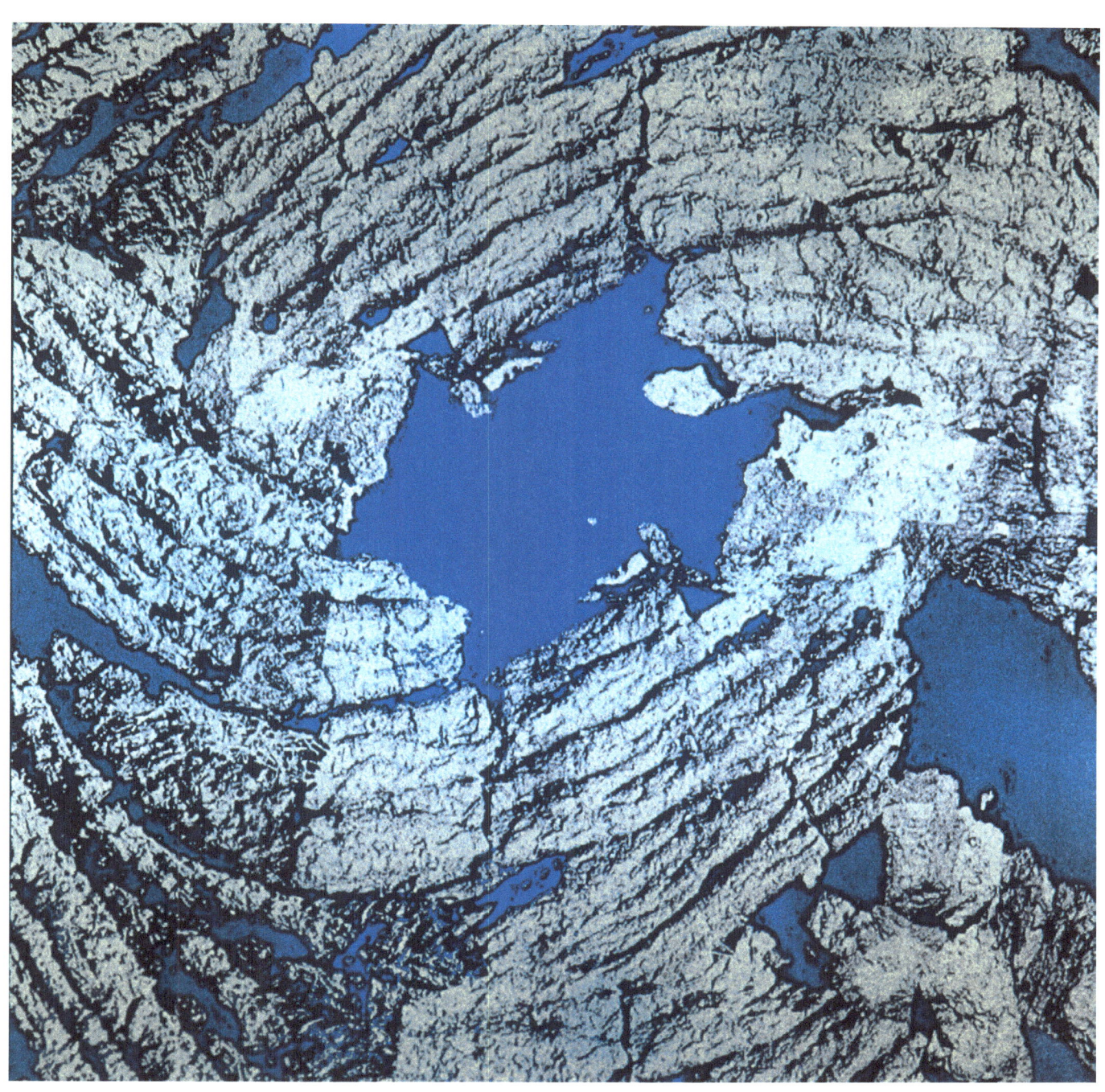

Fractal 20 , *viscosity solarplate etching, 24 x24 inches*

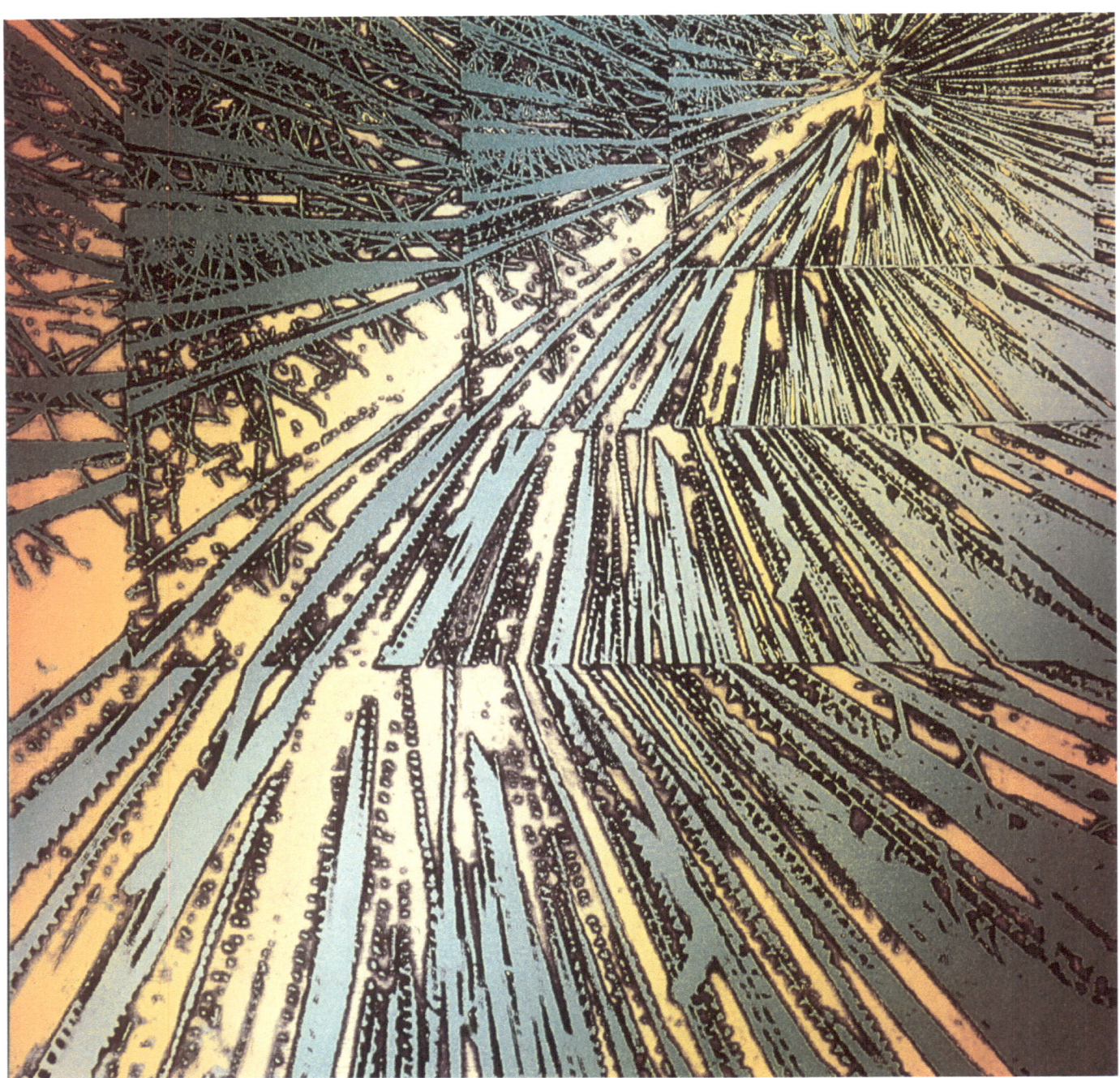

Fractal 28, *viscosity solarplate etching, 18 x18 inches*

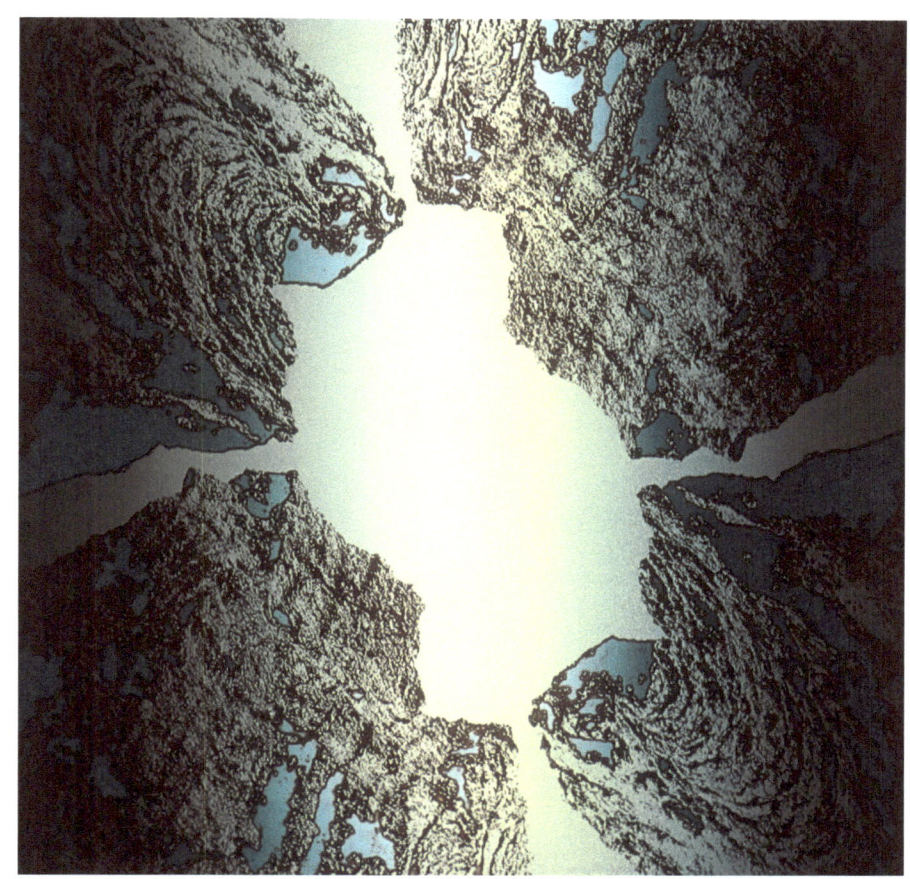

Fractal 22, *viscosity solarplate etching, 24 x 24 inches*

Fractal 26, *viscosity solarplate etching, 18 x 18 inches*

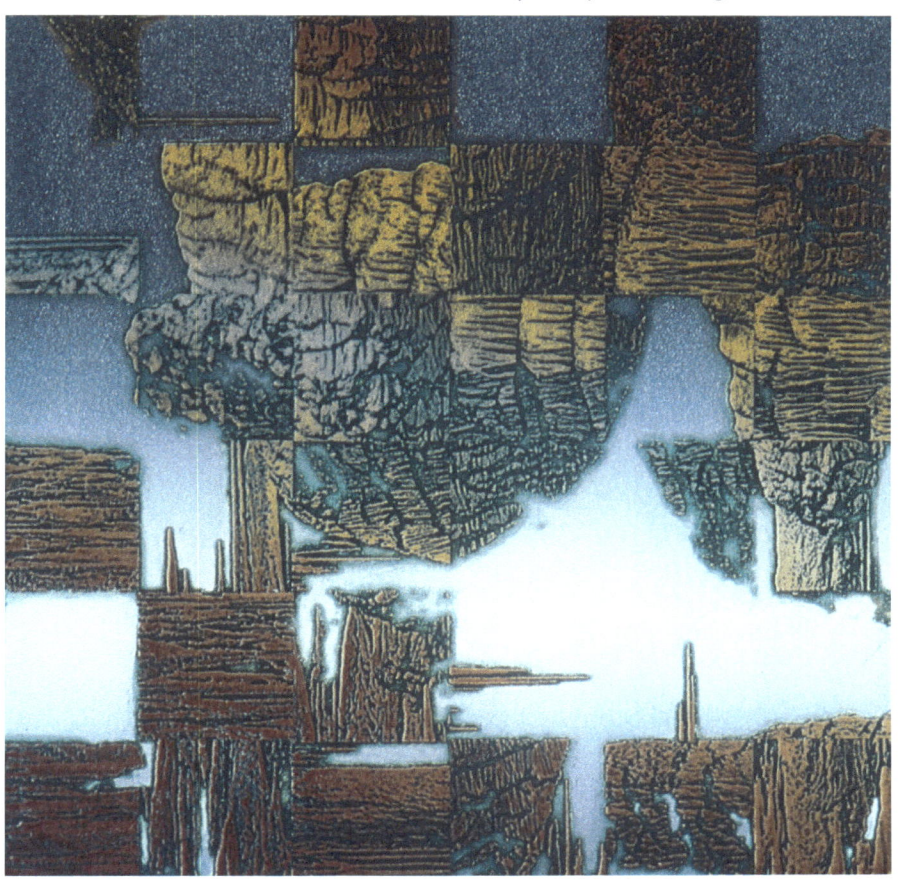

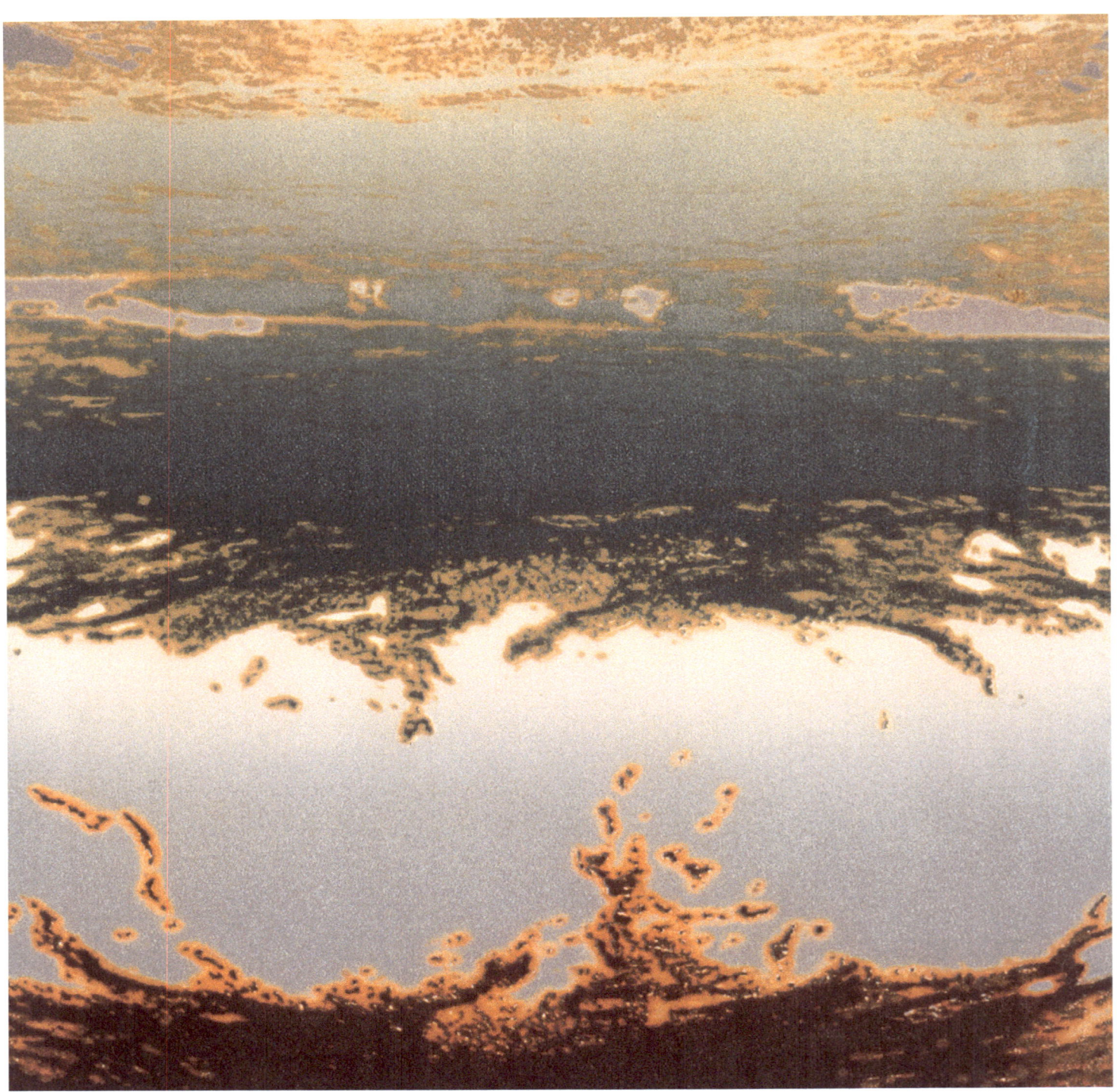

Fractal 38, *viscosity solarplate etching, 18 x 18 inches*

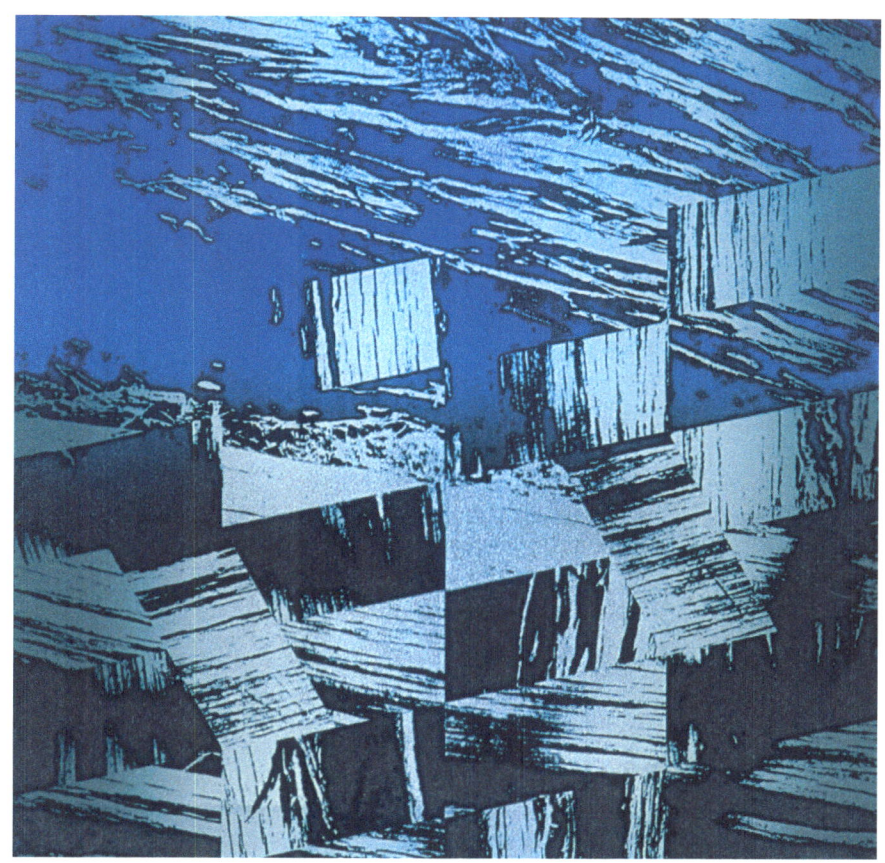

Fractal 21, *viscosity solarplate etching, 24 x 24 inches*

Fractal 23, *viscosity solarplate etching, 24 x 24 inches*

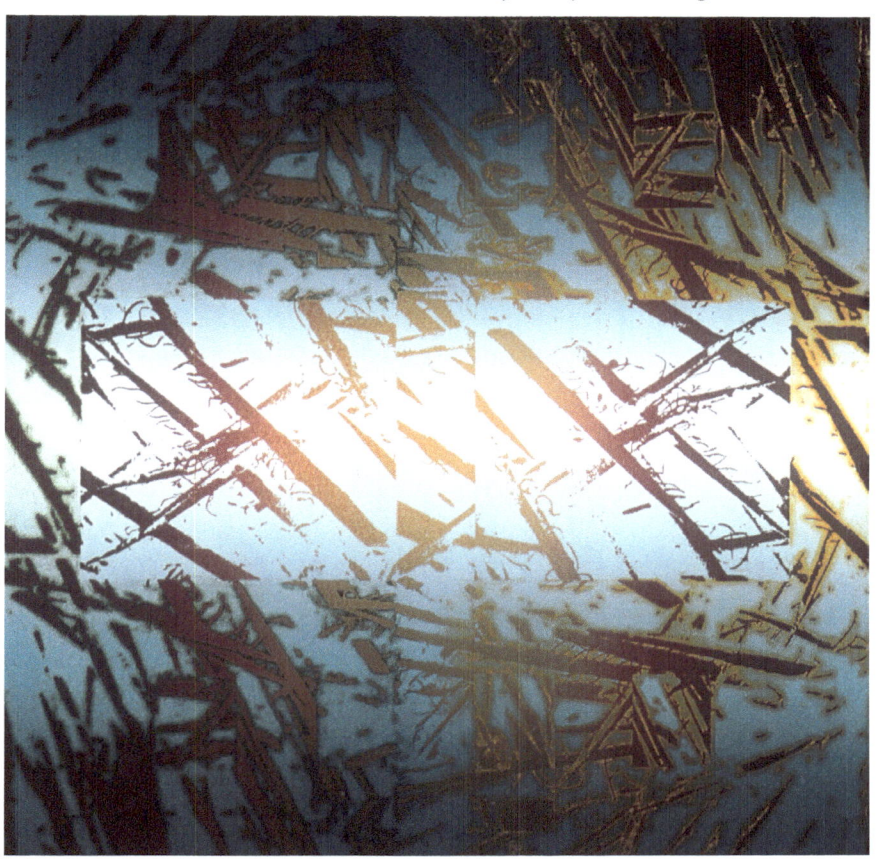

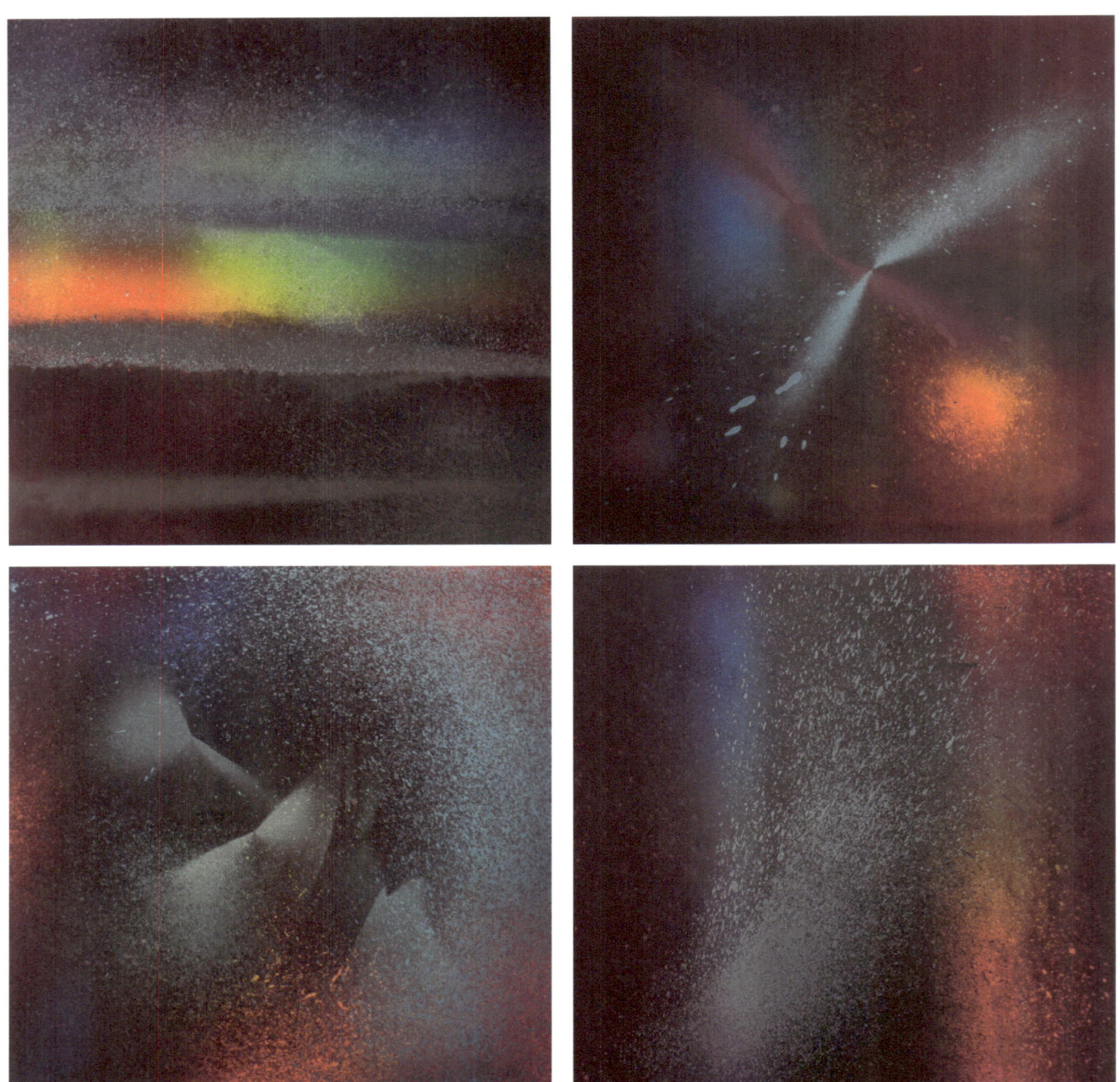

CL Series (clockwise from upper left) #1, #3, #2, #7, *reverse aquatint and aquatint, 20 x 20 inches each*

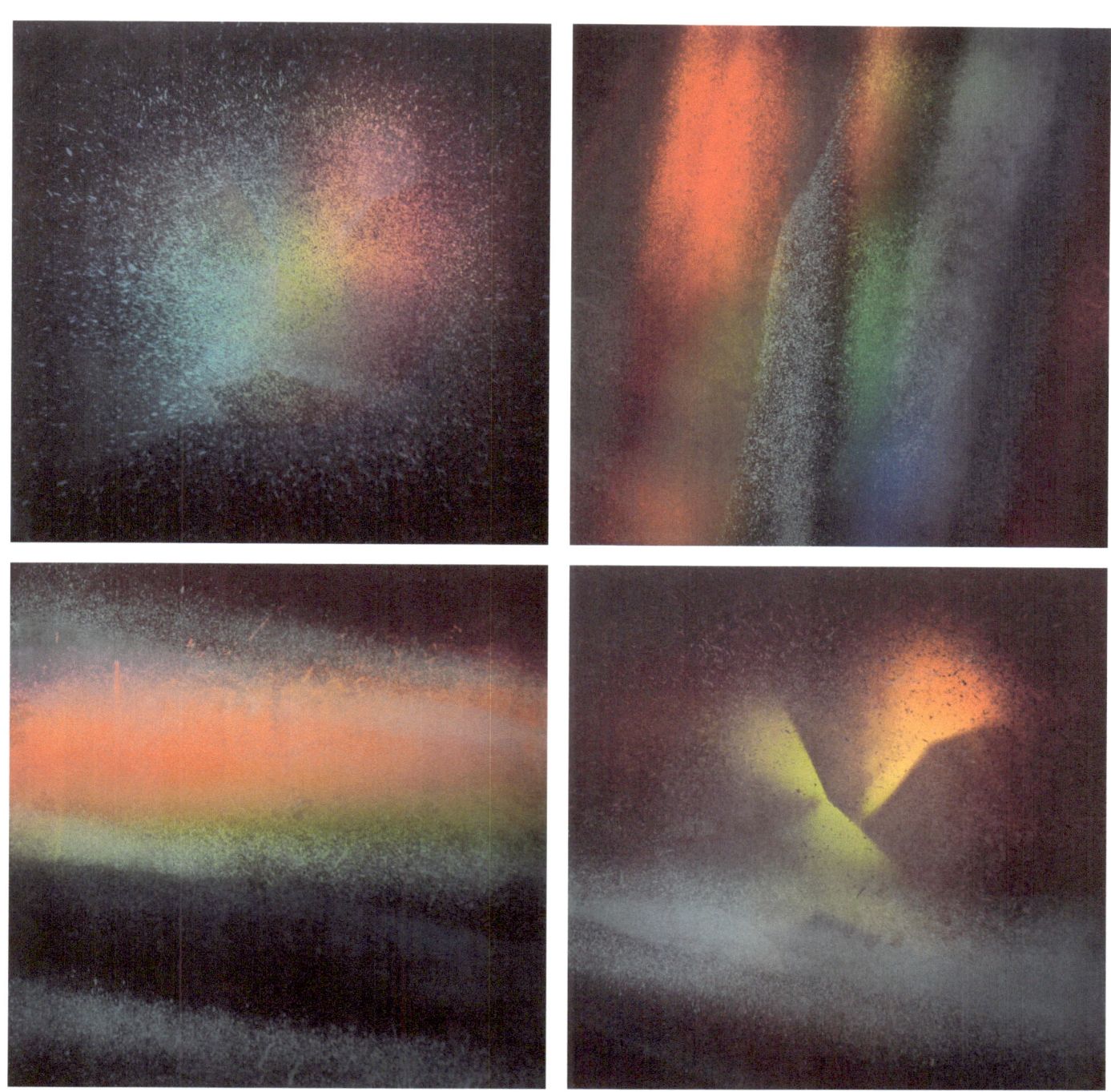

CL Series (clockwise from upper left) #8, #12, #4, #6, *reverse aquatint and aquatint, 20 x 20 inches each*

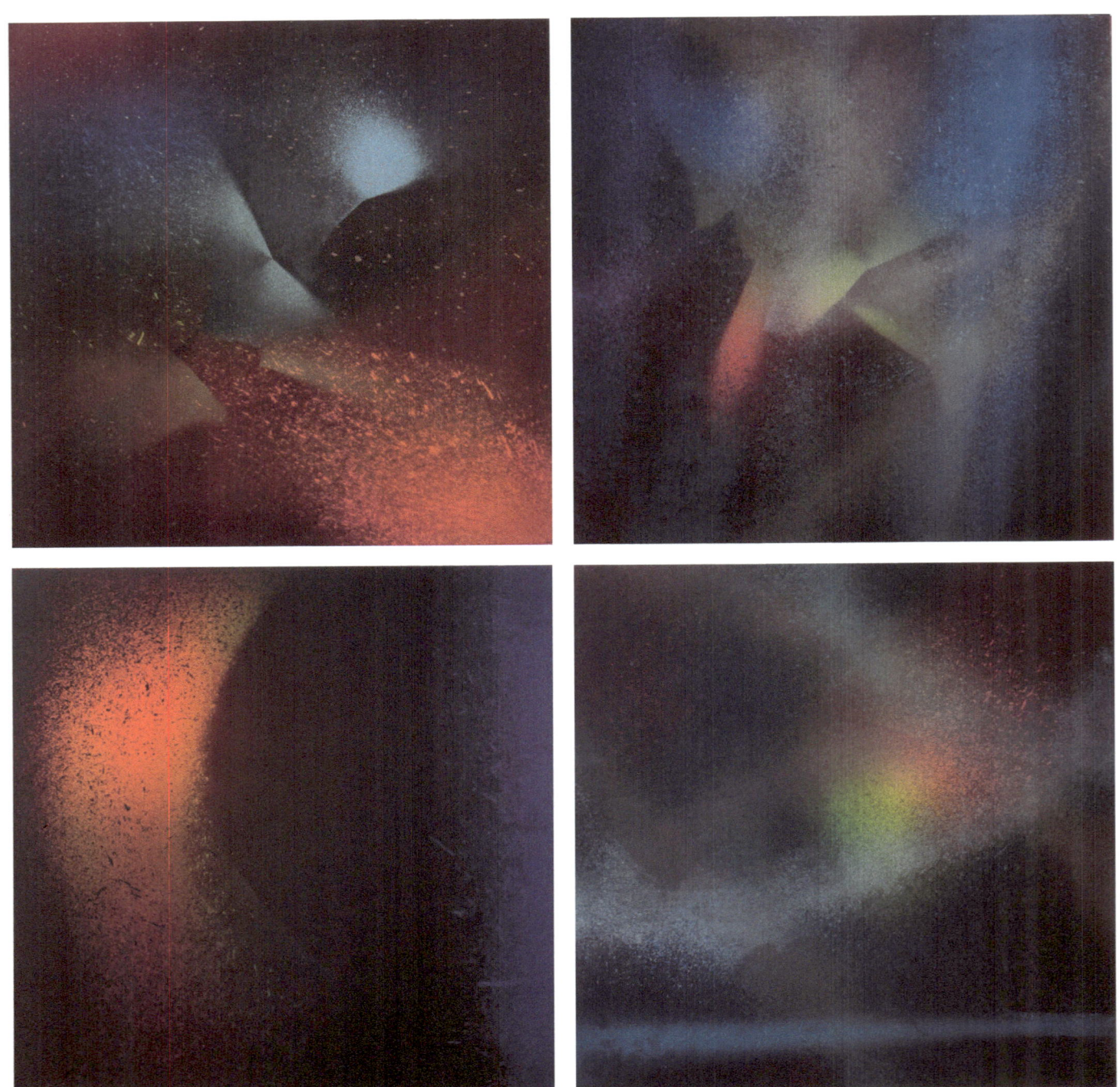

CL Series (clockwise from upper left) #5, #13, #14, #10, *reverse aquatint and aquatint, 20 x 20 inches each*

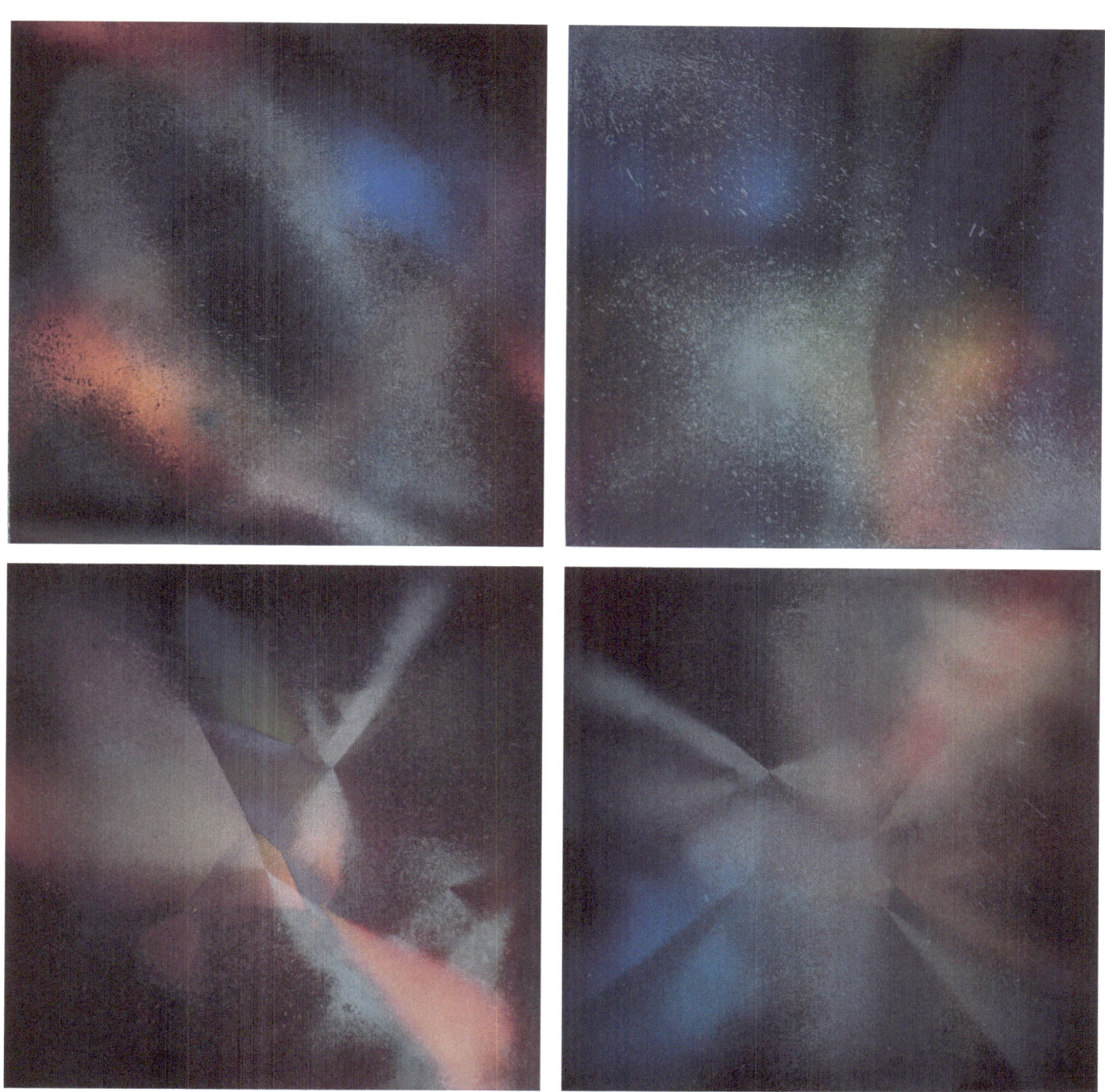

CL Series (clockwise from upper left) #15, #16, #12B, #11, *reverse aquatint and aquatint, 20 x 20 inches each*

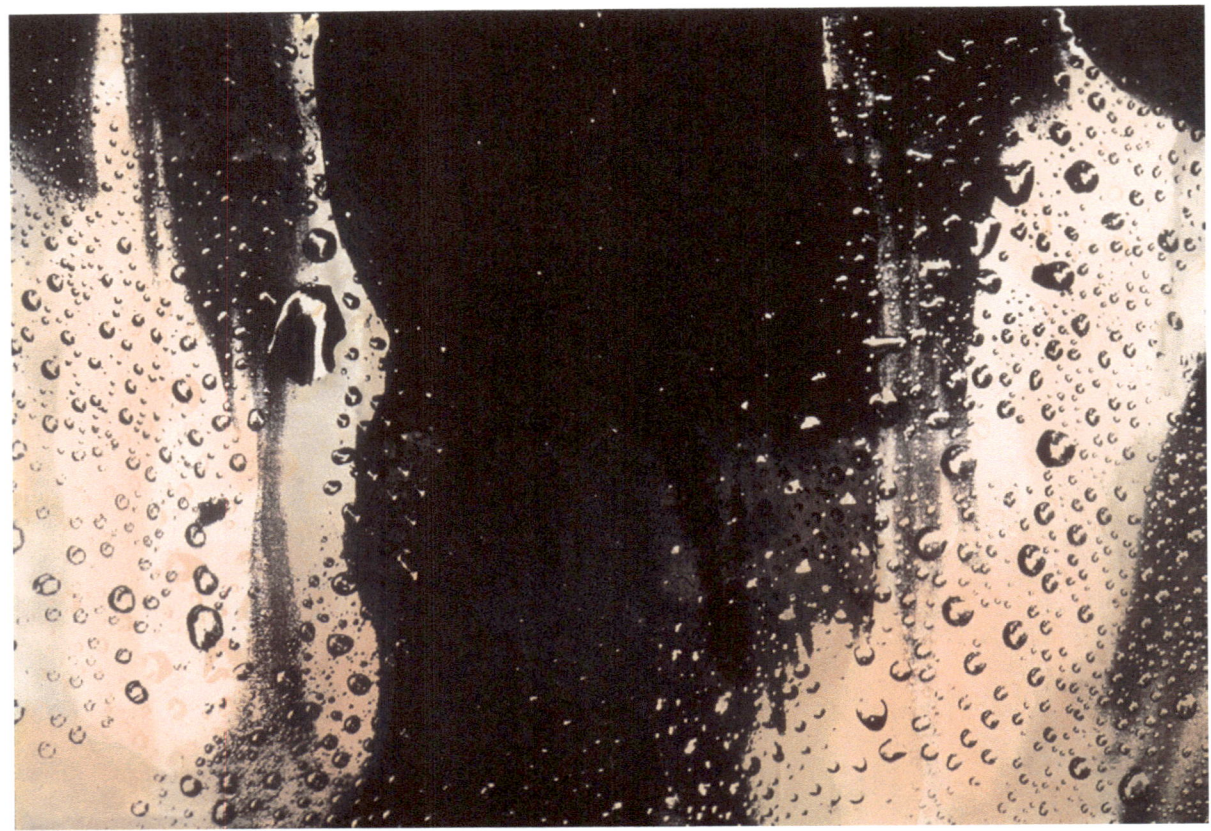

L 21, *polyester plate lithograph, 40 x 54 inches. Photo: Pat Pollard*

L 26, *polyester plate lithograph, 54 x 40 inches. Photo: Pat Pollard*

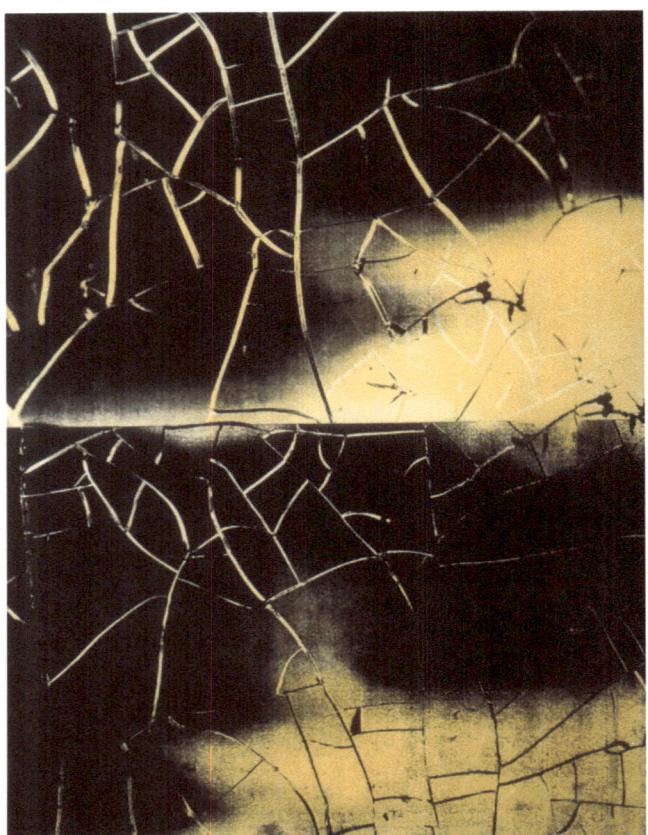

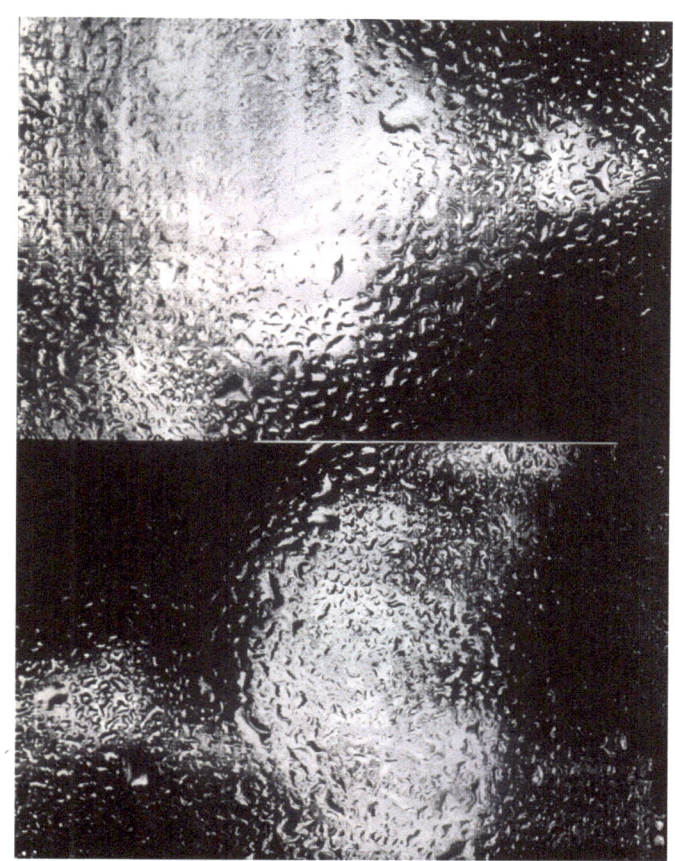

L 21, polyester plate lithograph, 54 x 40 inches. Photo: Pat Pollard

L 16, polyester plate lithograph, 40 x 54 inches. Photo: Pat Pollard

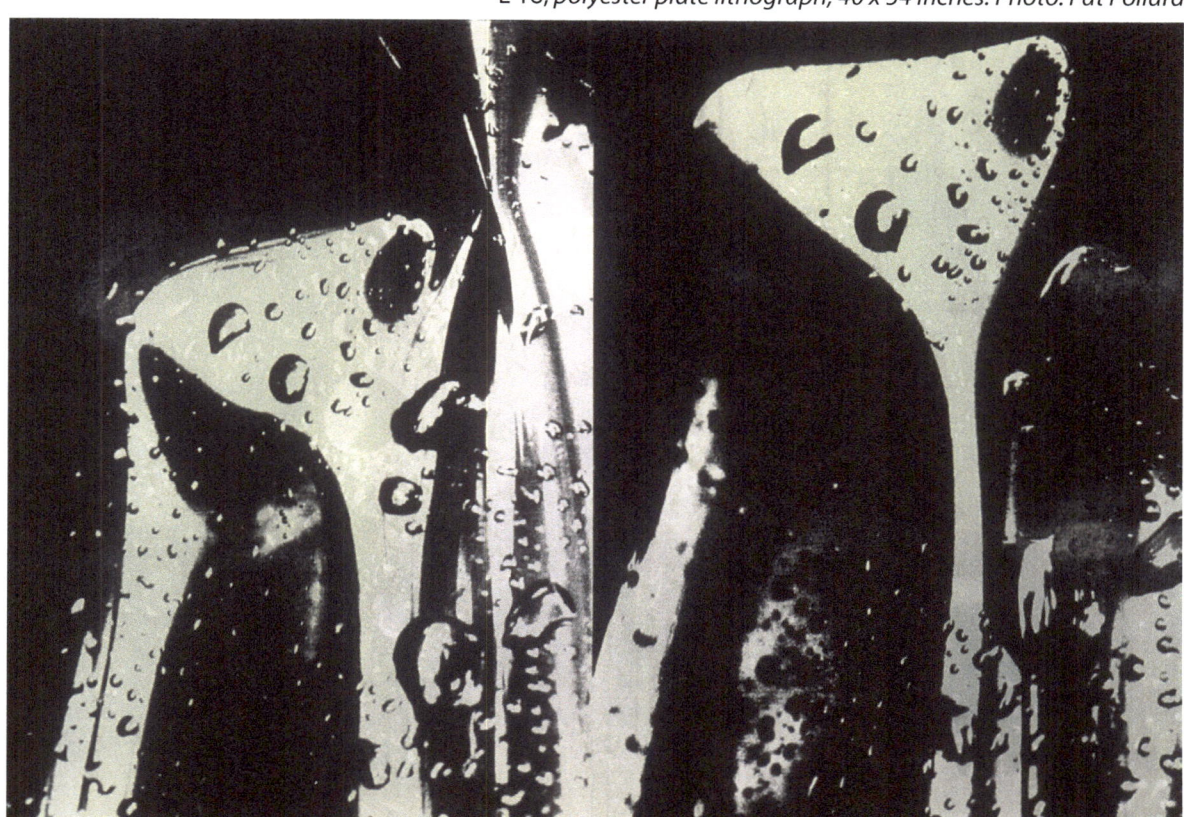

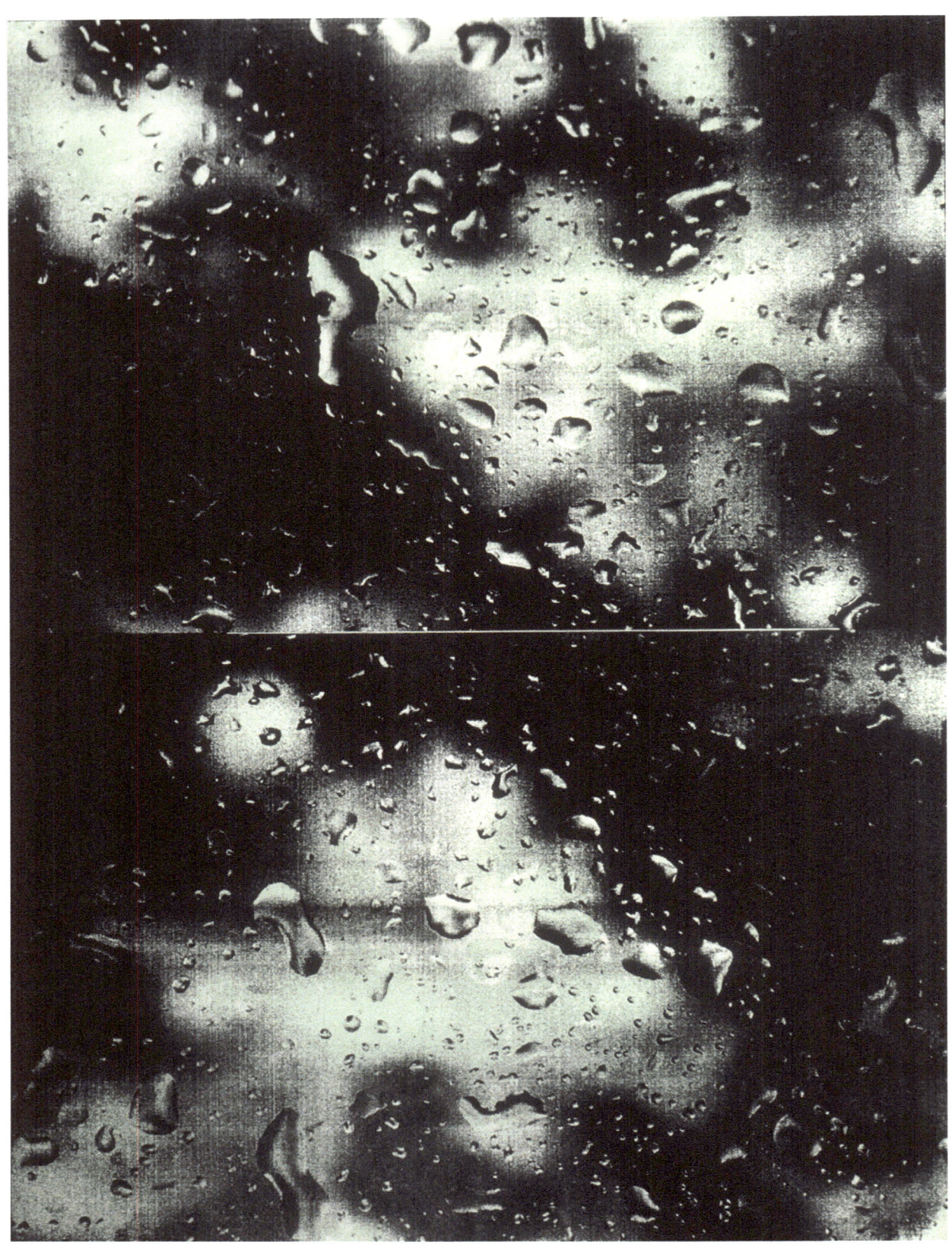

L 2, *polyester plate lithograph, 54 x 40 inches. Photo: Pat Pollard*

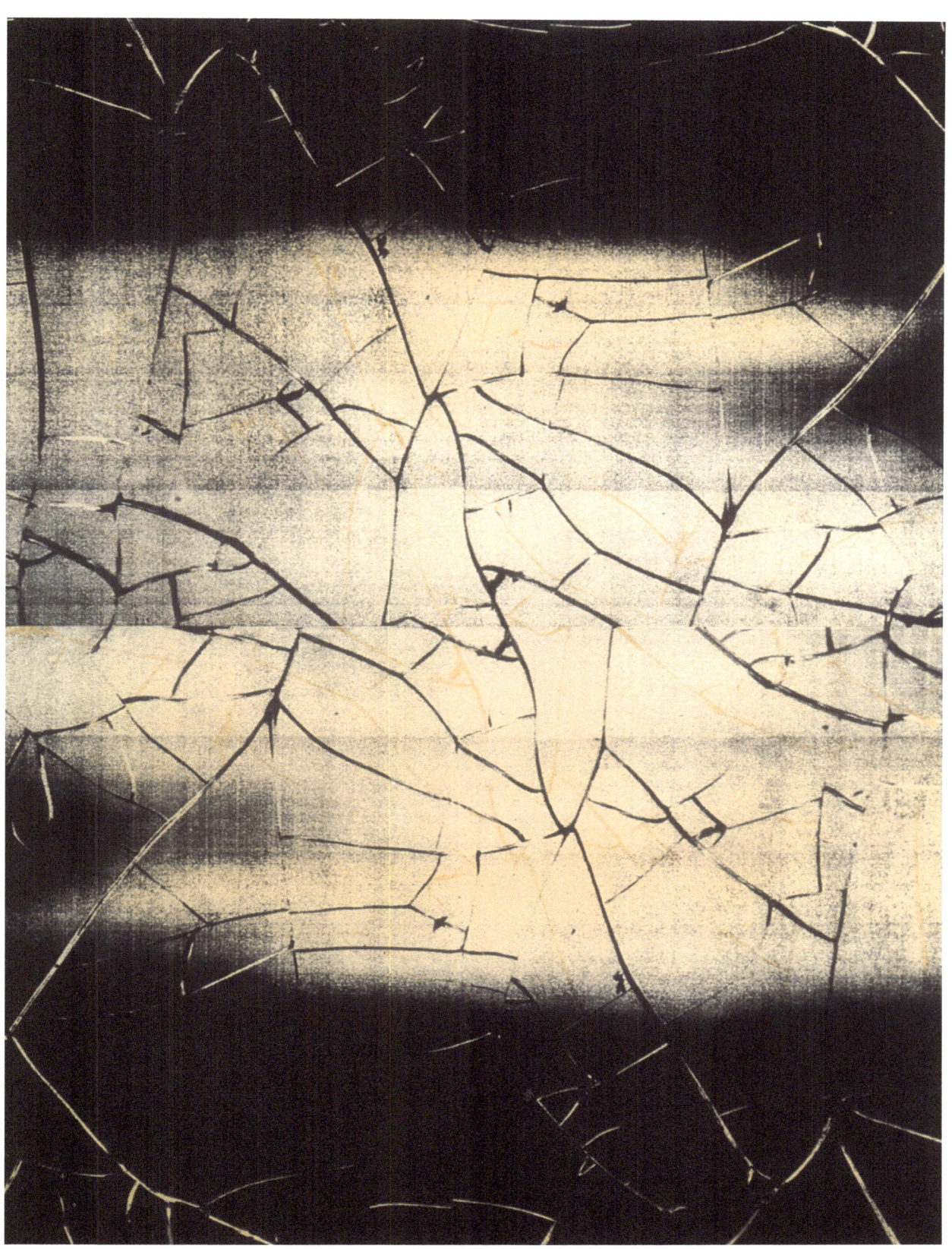

L 9, polyester plate lithograph, 54 x 40 inches. Photo: Pat Pollard

Mitchell Marti

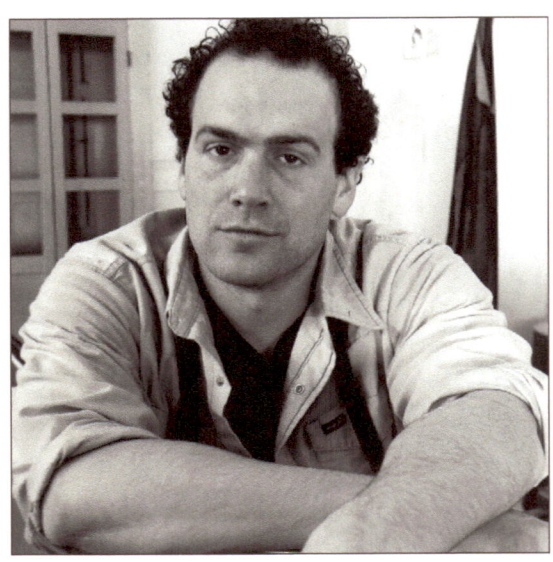

Mitchell Marti's mixed media prints, utilizing lithography, relief, woodblock, etching, and photographic techniques are so interwoven in their creative generation that very few printmakers would even attempt to match them. The happy surprise is that the freshness, and uplifting color of these prints shines effortlessly through the complexity. Mr. Marti is the owner and master printer of Interbang Press, a professional collaborative printmaking studio located in Santa Fe, NM.

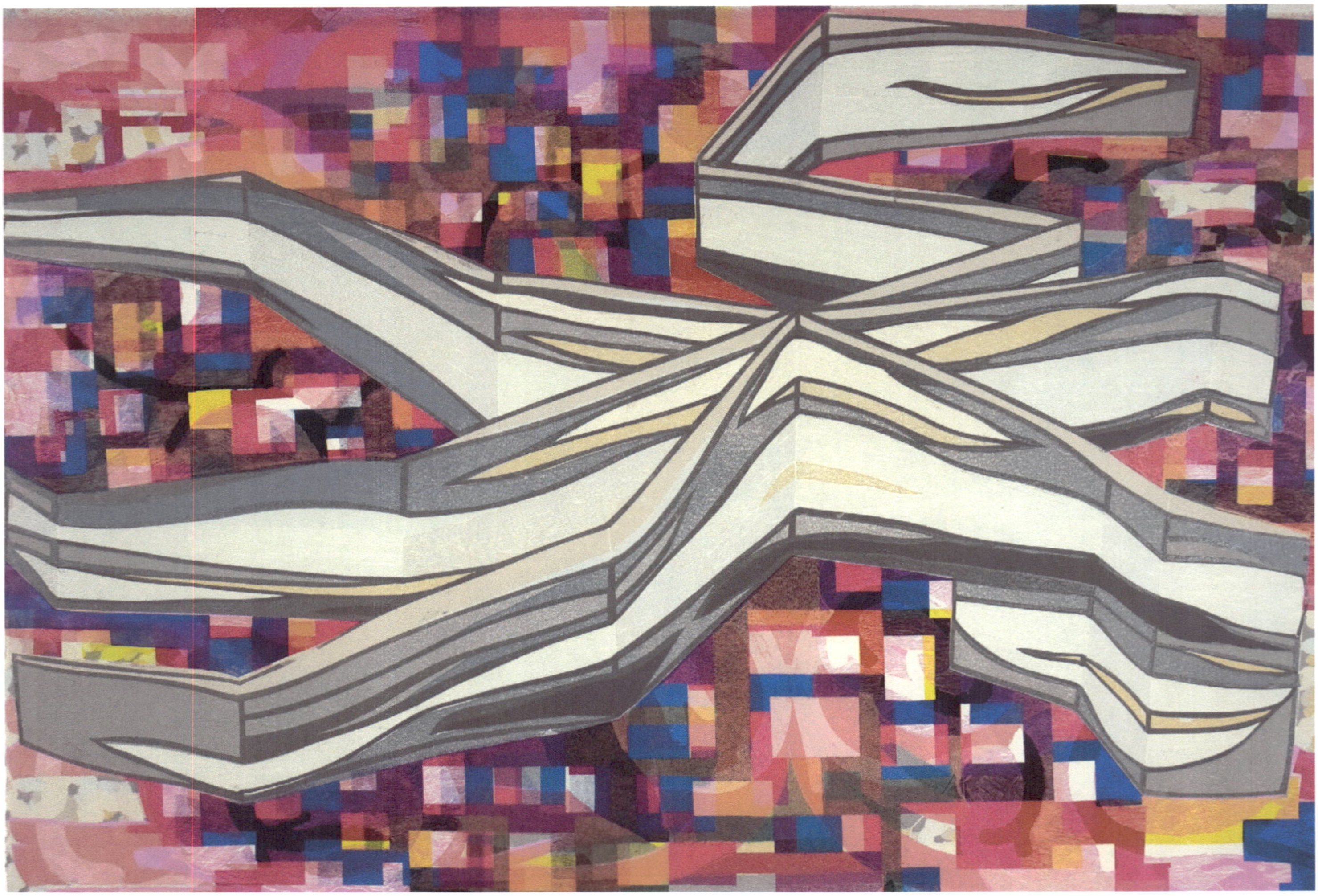

Generalized Section III, *woodcut, 34 x 46 inches*

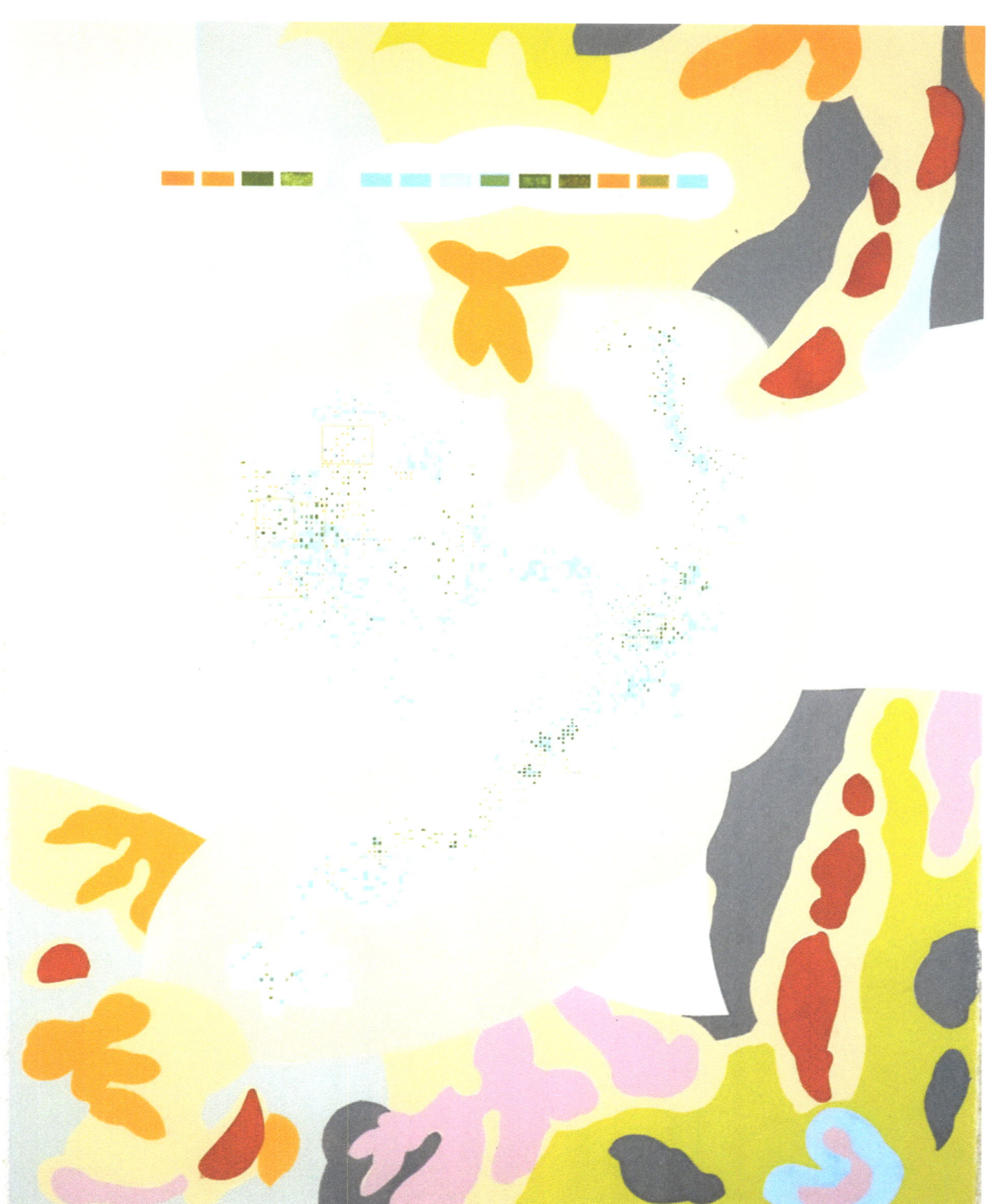

Data Miner, *lithography and relief, 30 x 22 inches*

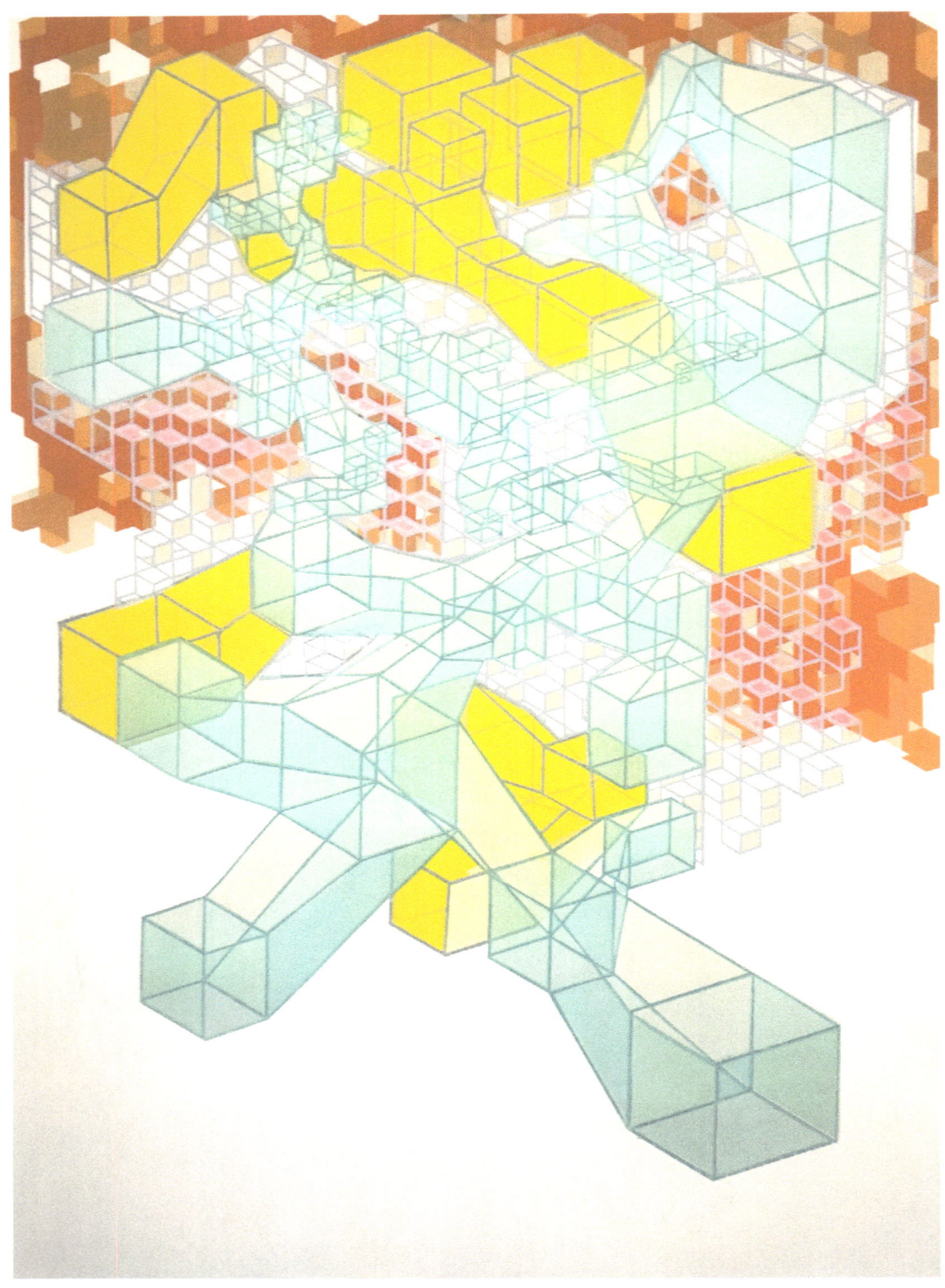

Known and Projected Quantities, *woodcut, 51 x 38 inches*

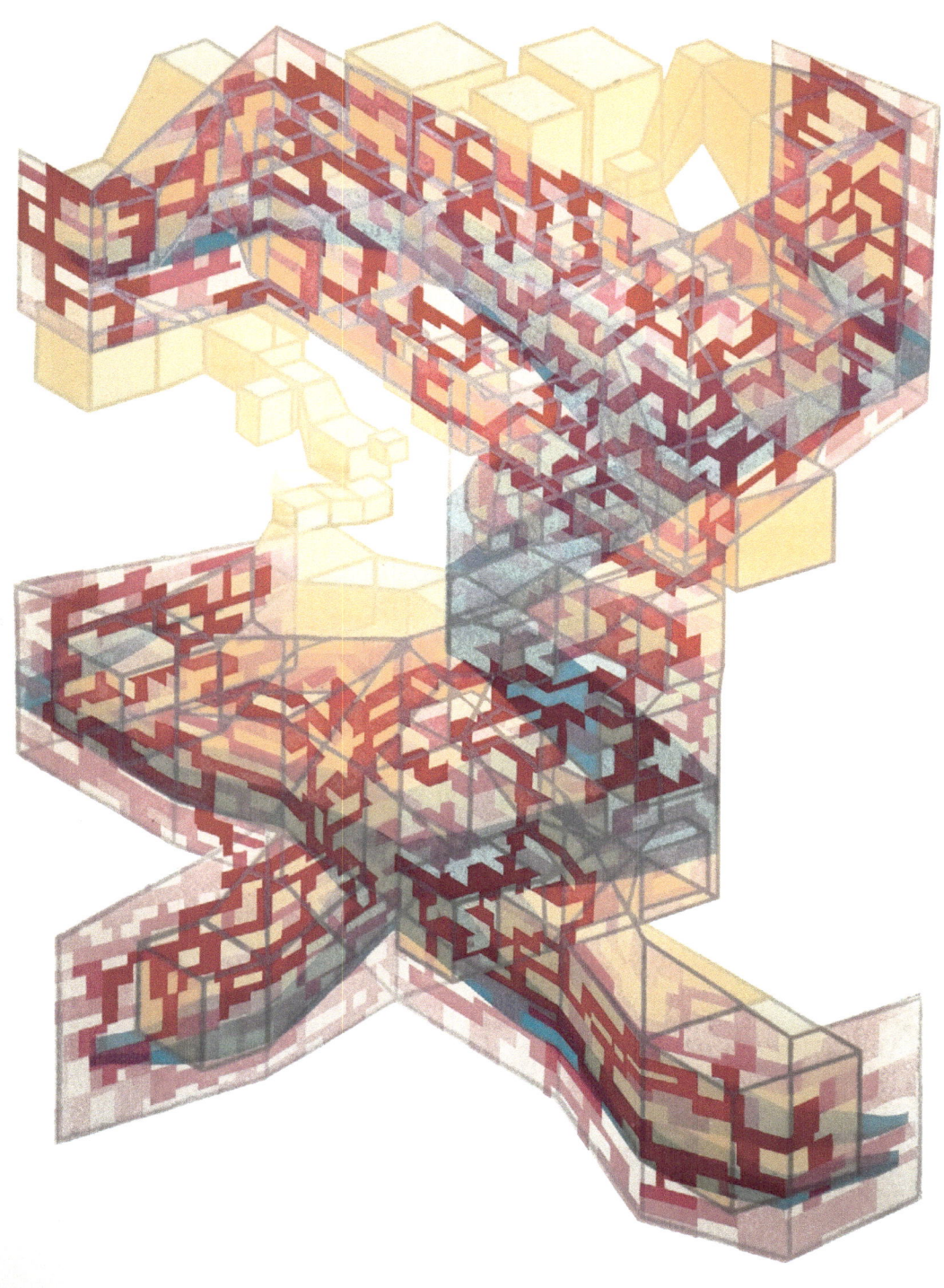

Interference, *woodcut, 51 x 38 inches*

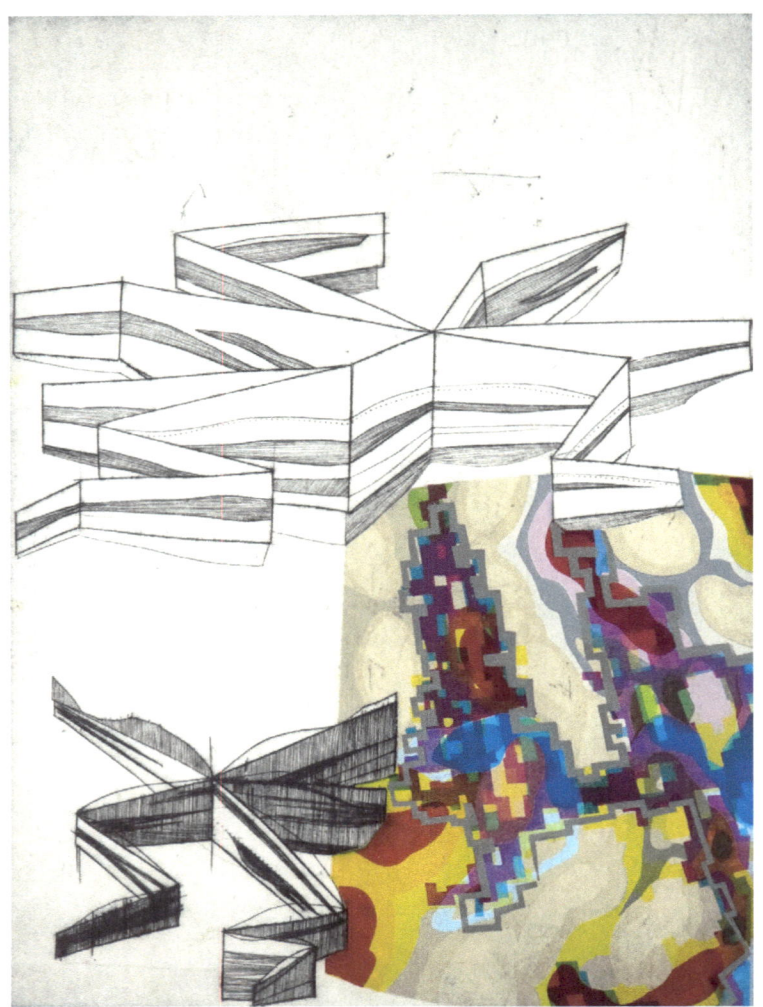

Generalized Section I, *intaglio and relief, 16 ½ x 13 inches*

Generalized Section II, *intaglio and relief, 19 x 25 inches*

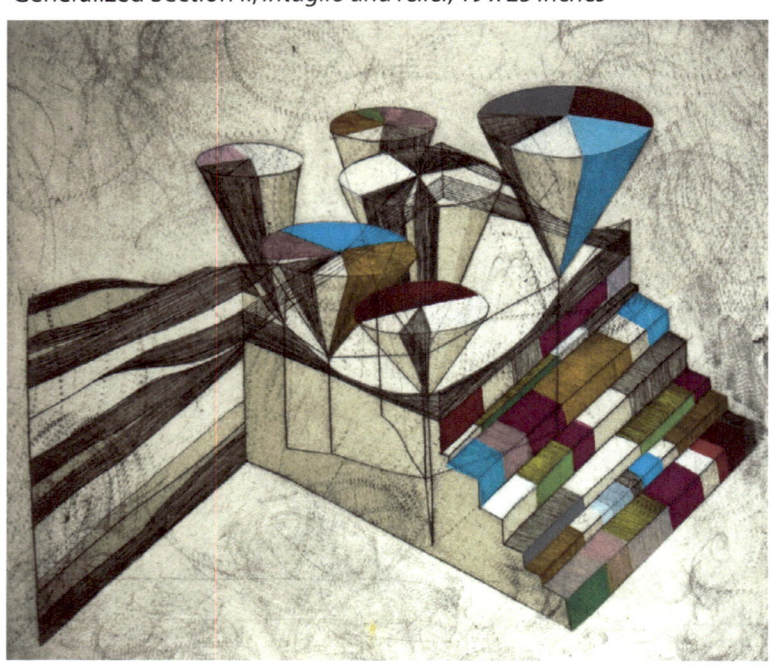

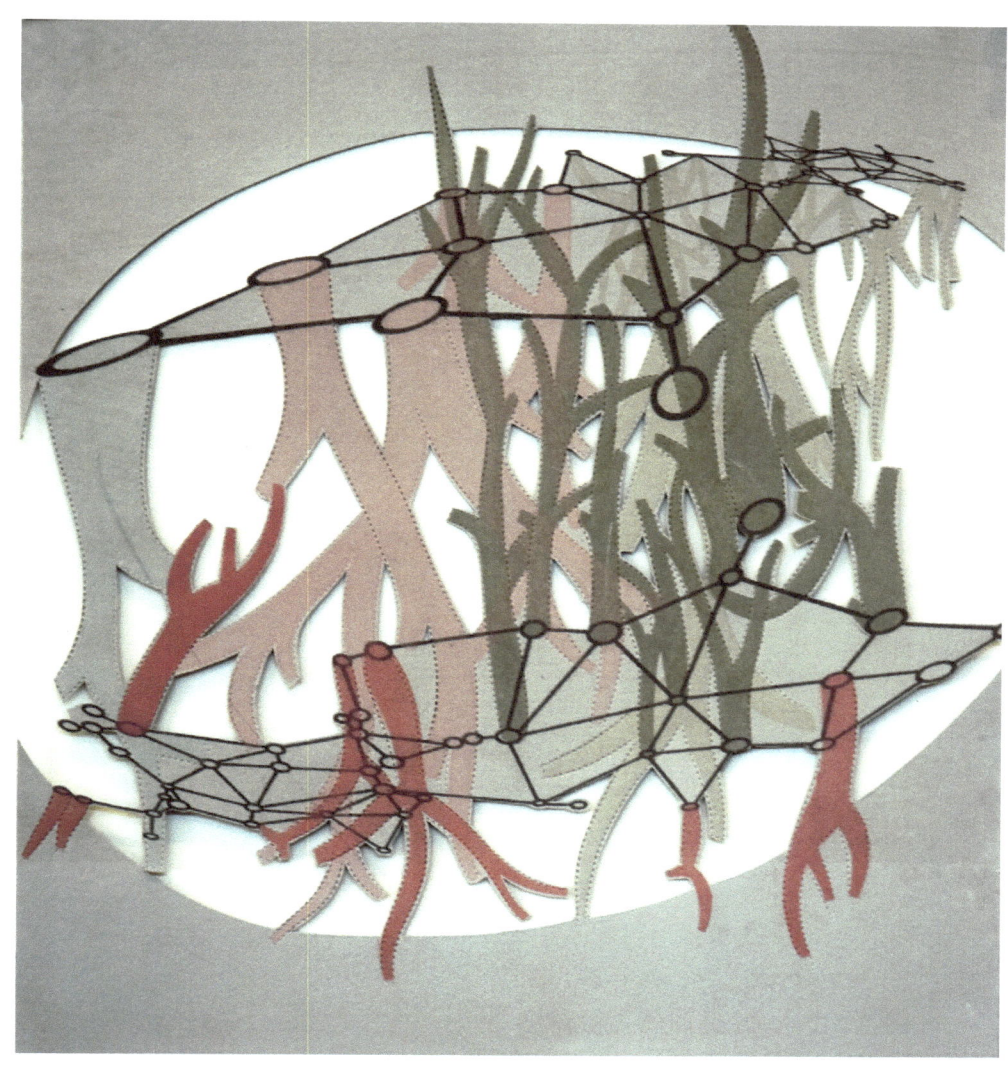

Sweet Crude II, *lithography and relief, 17 x 16 inches*

Sweet Crude, *lithography and relief, 17 x 15 inches*

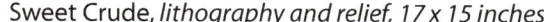

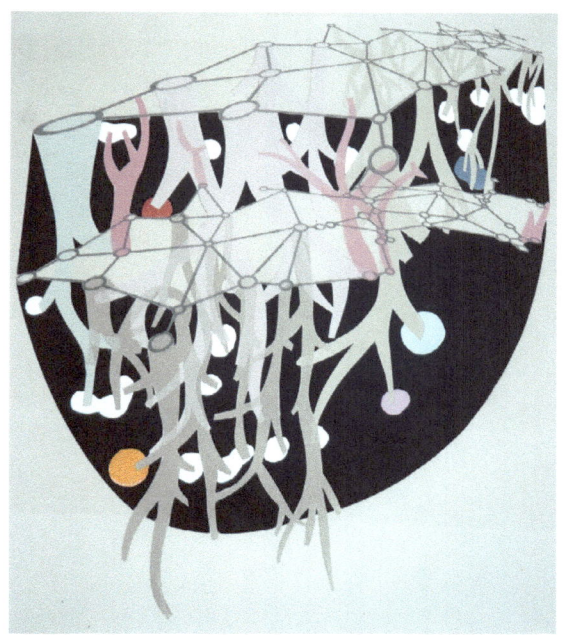

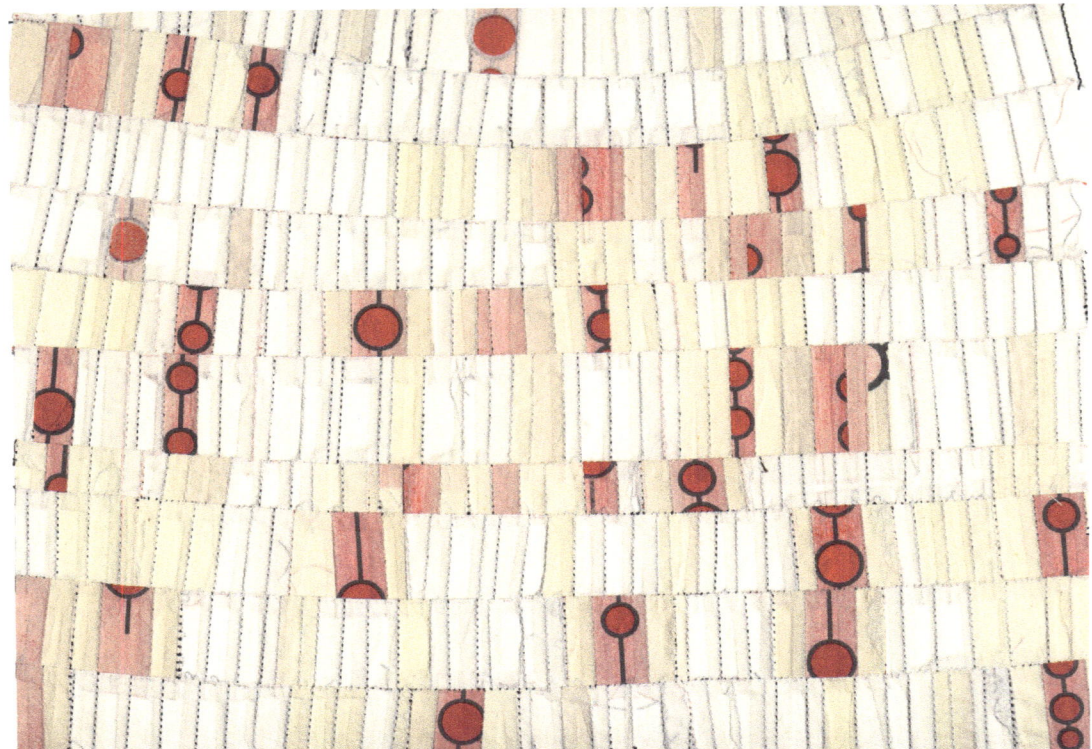

Oil Patch Work Quilt, *lithography, chine collé, 24 x 29 inches*

The Patch II, *lithography, chine collé, 24 x 29 inches*

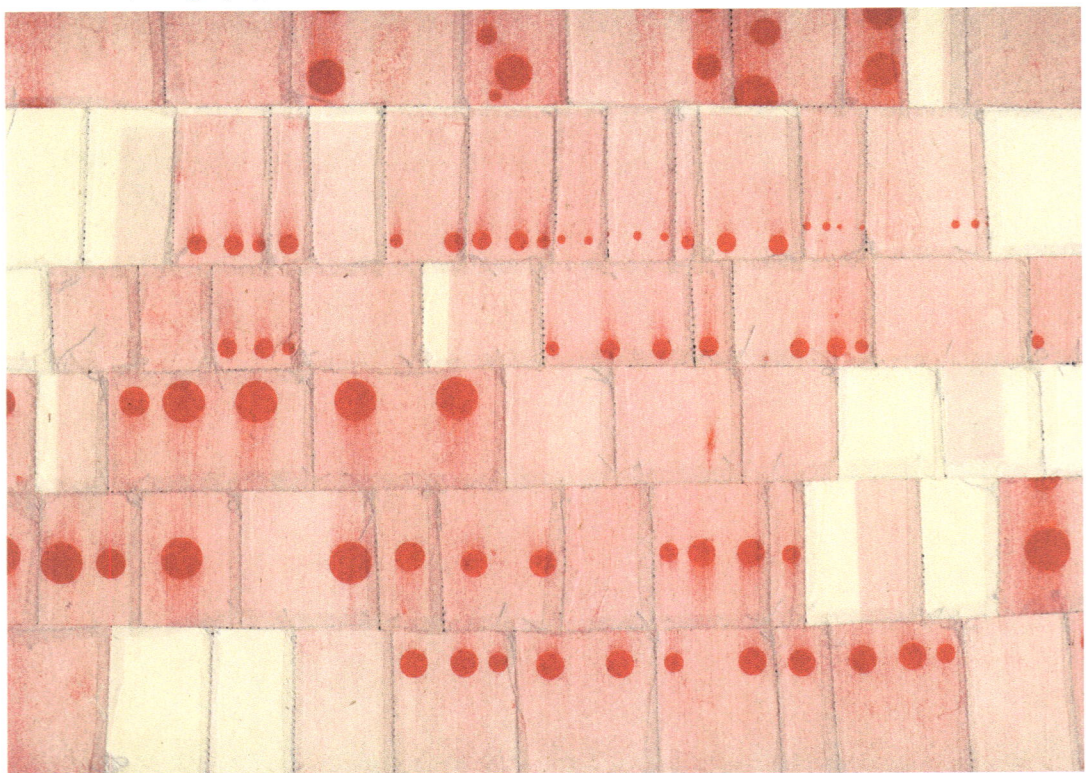

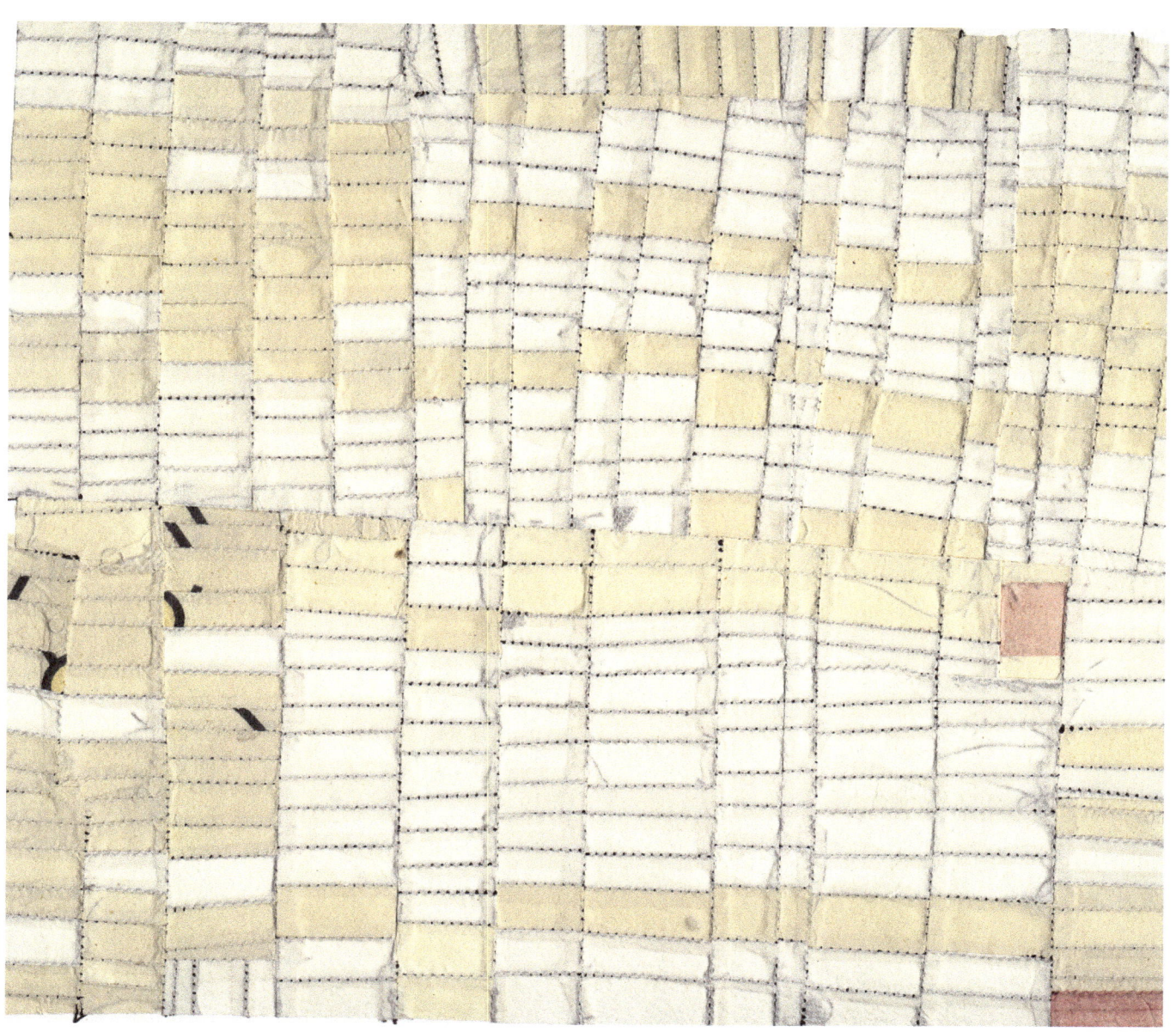

The Patch III, *lithography, chine collé, 24 x 29 inches*

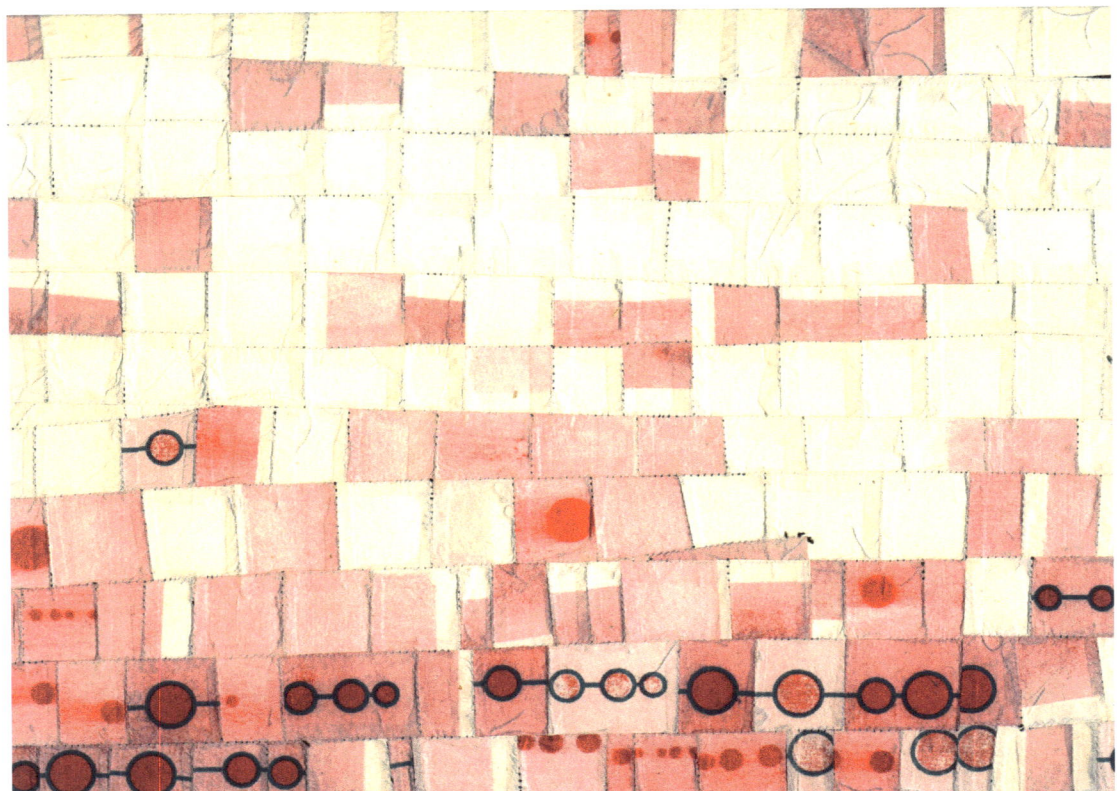

The Patch V, *lithography, chine collé, 24 x 29 inches*

The Patch VI, *lithography, chine collé, 24 x 29 inches*

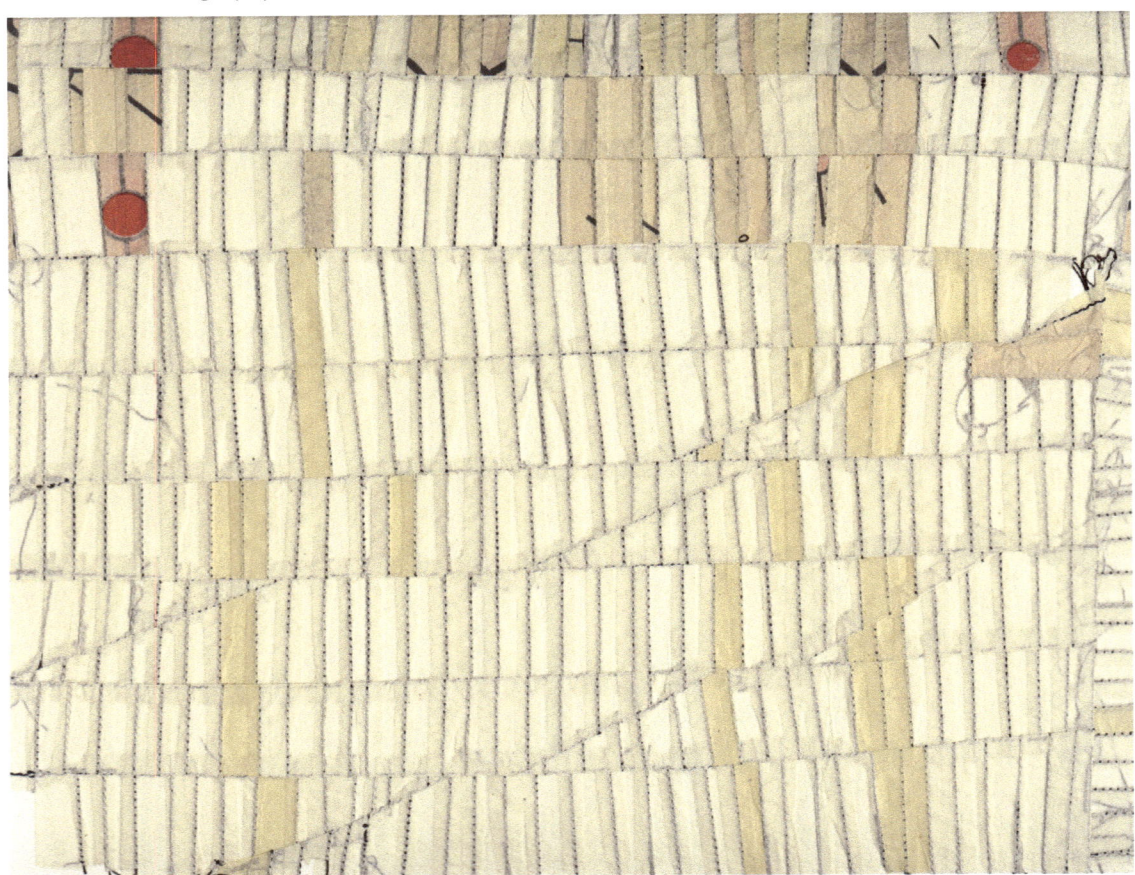

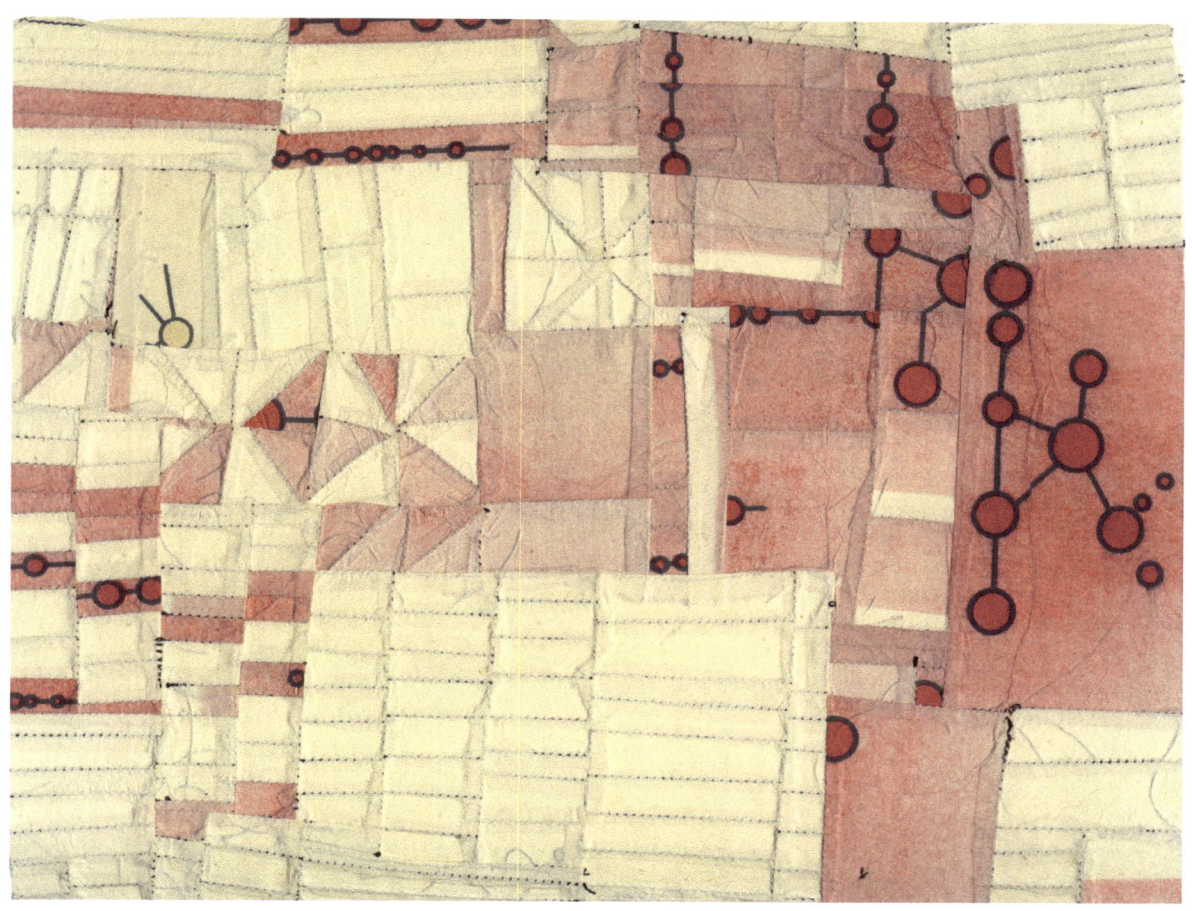

The Patch VII, *lithography, chine collé, 24 x 29 inches*

The Patch IV, *lithography, chine collé, 24 x 29 inches*

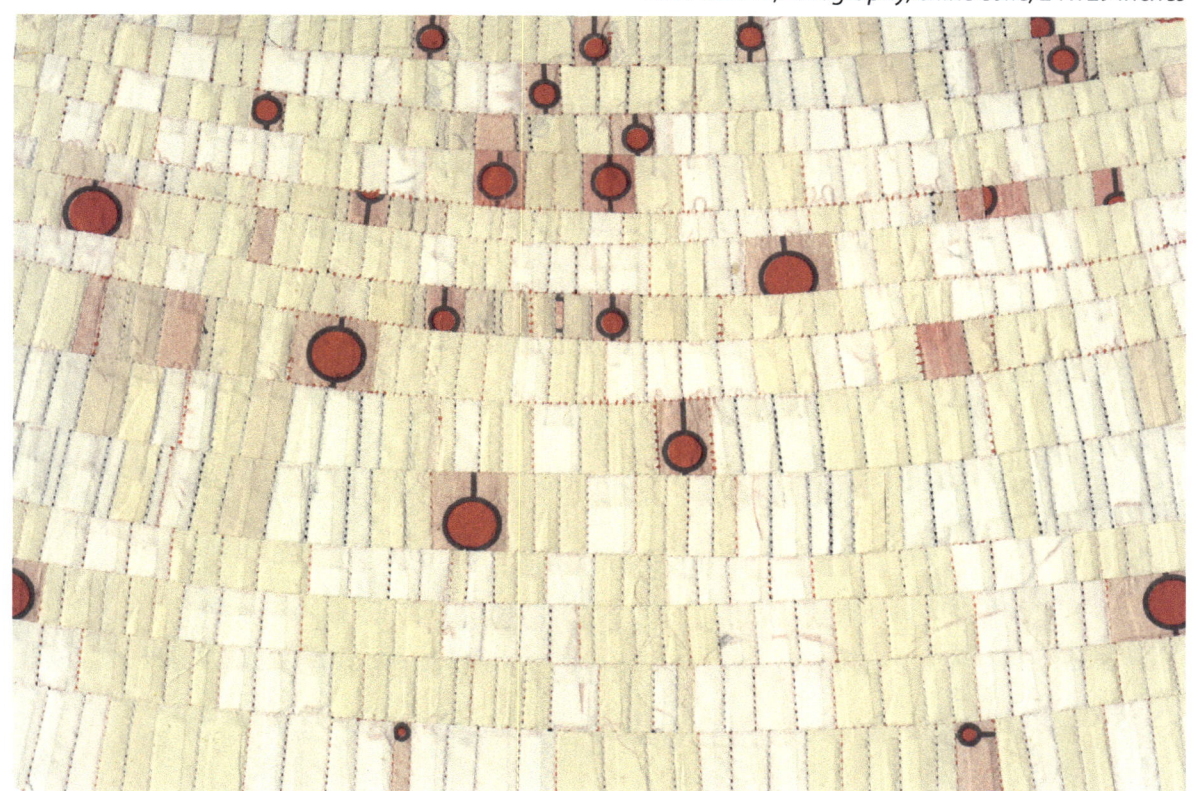

Michael Costello

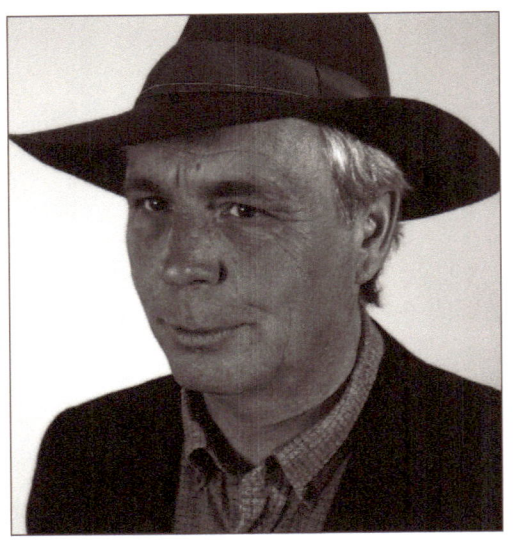

Michael Costello works with photography and film, and with glass, but also with monotype and wax, and with digital printing on grained aluminum plates. The North Atlantic series, which show the sea and clouds from the perspective of an airplane's window, recall a sense of freedom experienced near the edge of the atmosphere. His work brings together techniques not usually combined in printmaking, with the intent of seeing and expressing the inner process of perceiving, to capture the moment and feeling of inspiration. Mr. Costello is the owner and master printer of Hand Graphics in Santa Fe, NM. Hand Graphics is a fine art printmaking establishment, including a professional frame-shop, and print gallery.

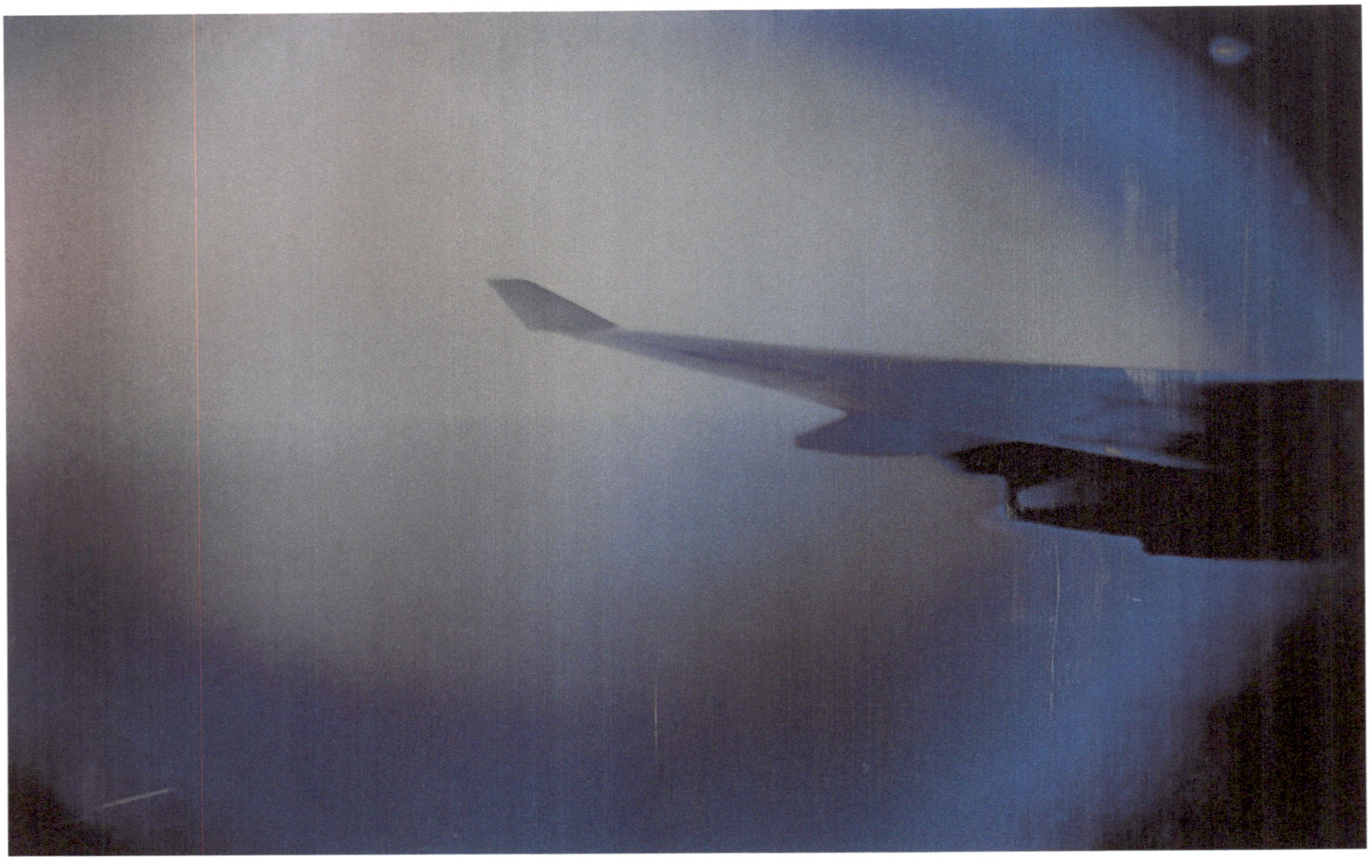

Wing, *monoprint, 25 x 37 inches*

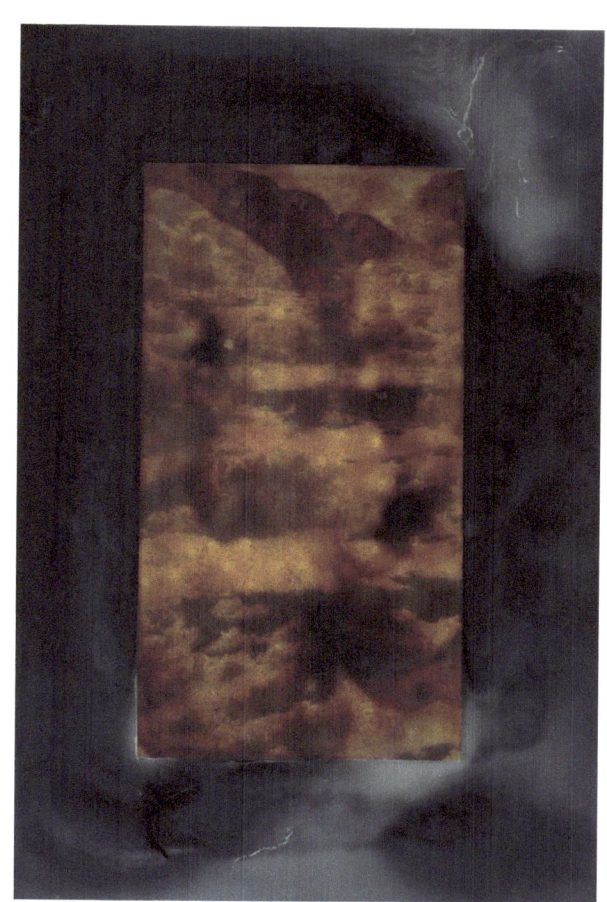

Ferric, *monoprint, 16 x 11*

Looking, *monoprint, beeswax, 11 x 9*

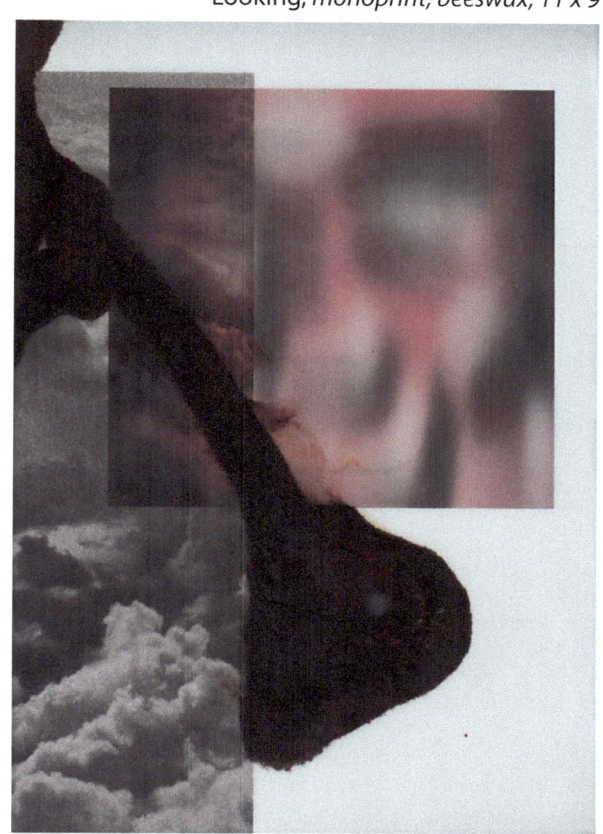

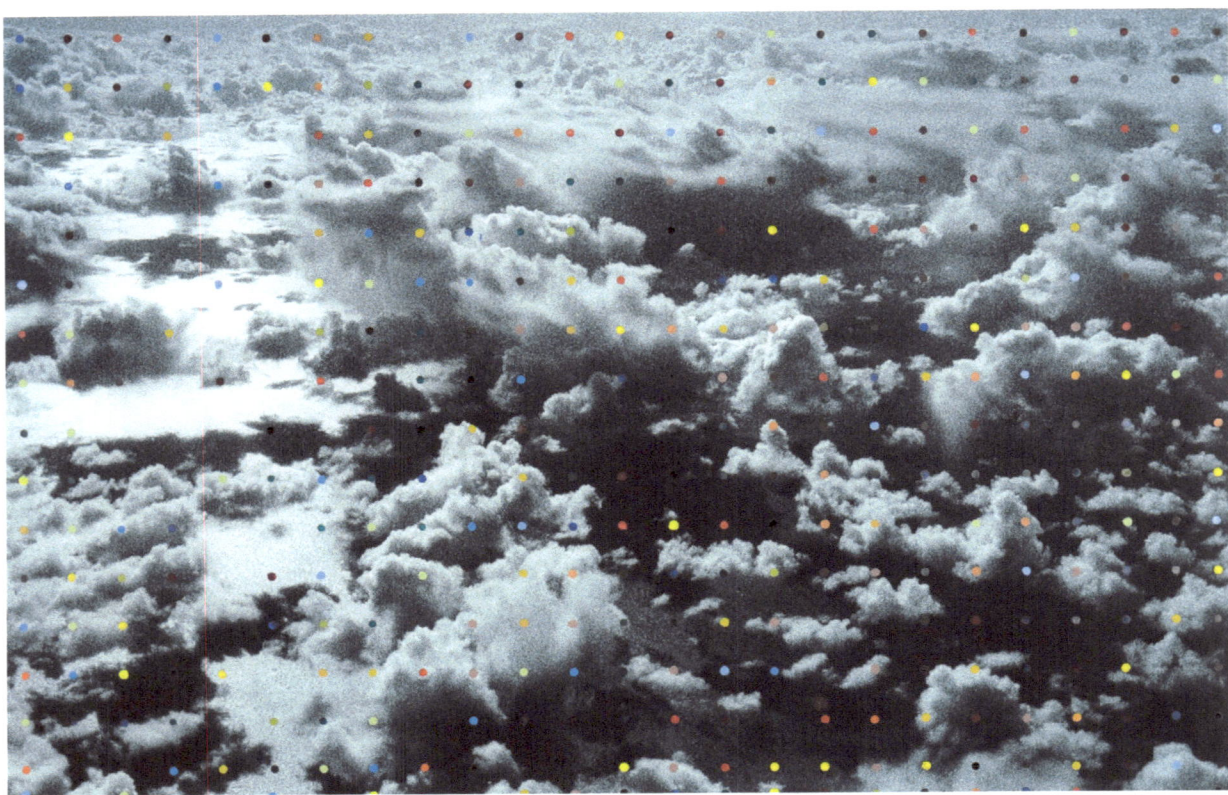

North Atlantic I, *monoprint, 25 x 40 inches*

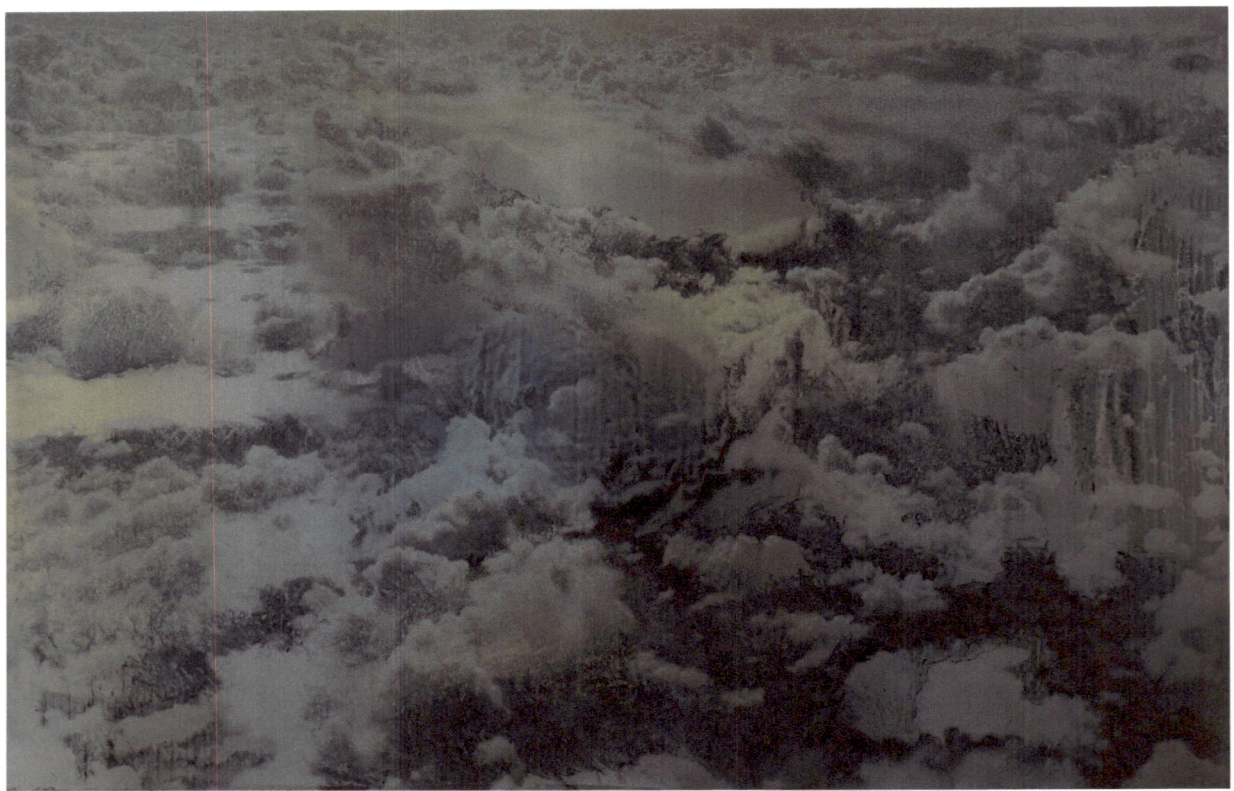

Turbulance Above The North Atlantic, *monoprint, 25 x 37*

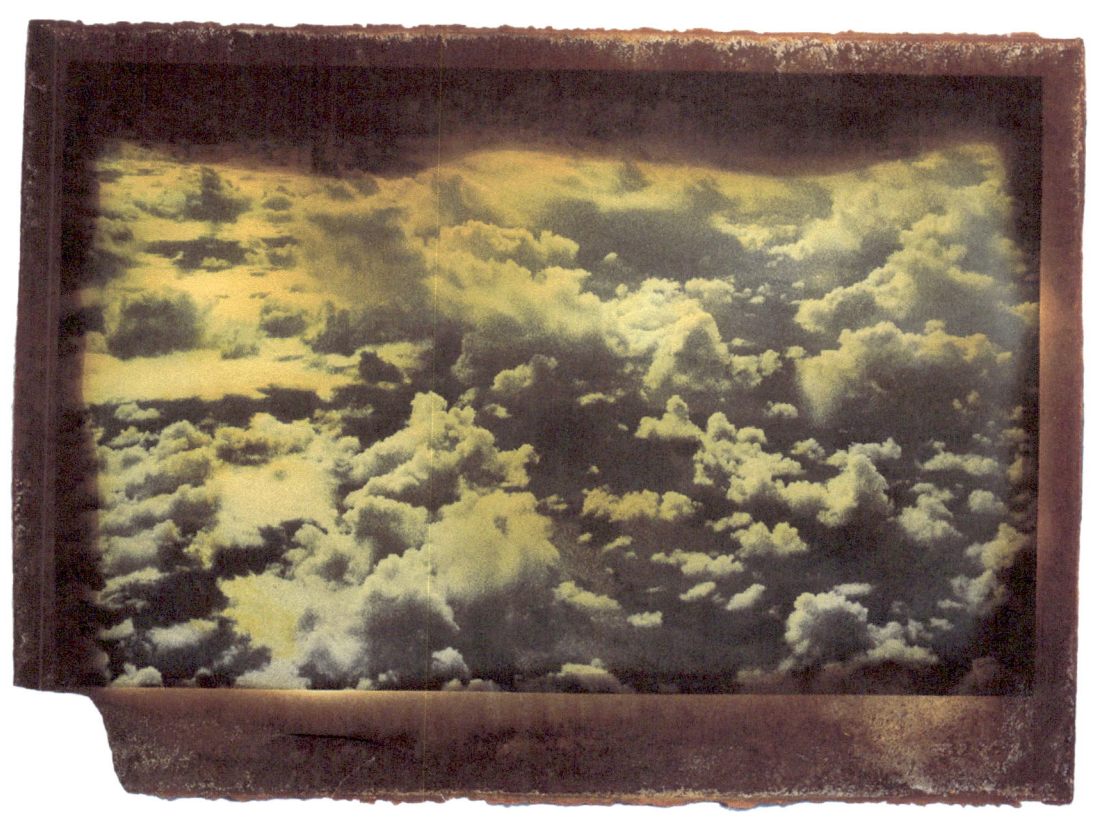

Rusting Clouds, *monoprint, 25 x 33 inches*

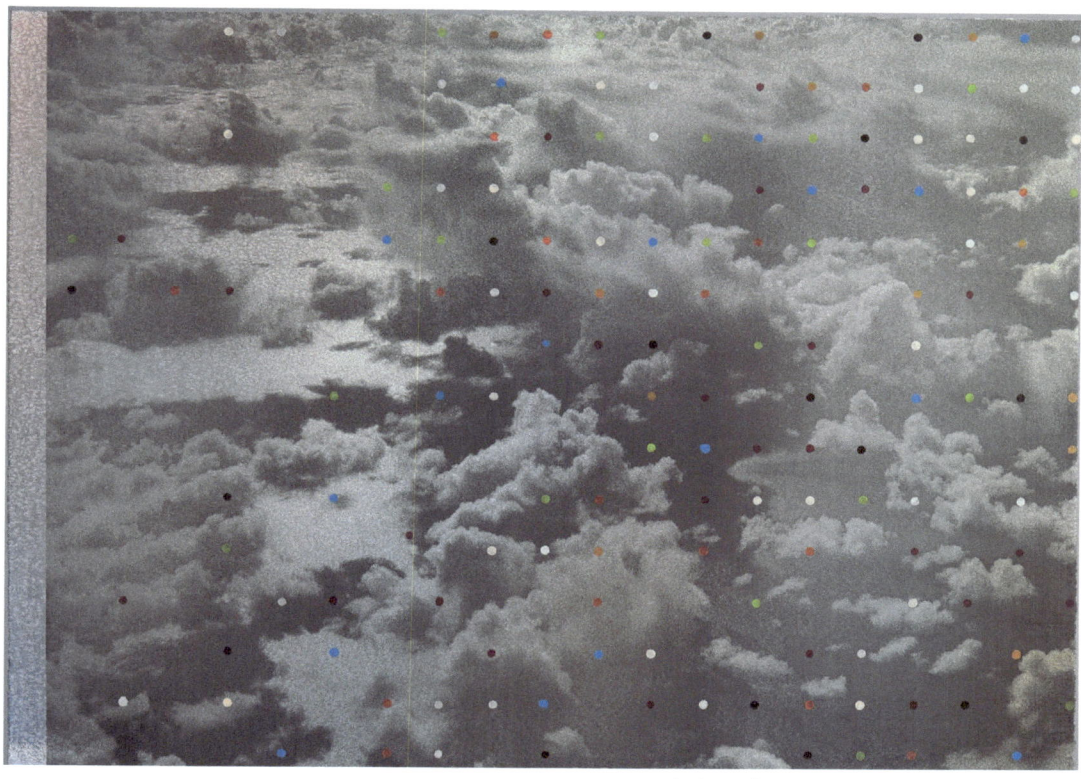

Irish Sea Plane, *monoprint, 25 x 33 inches*

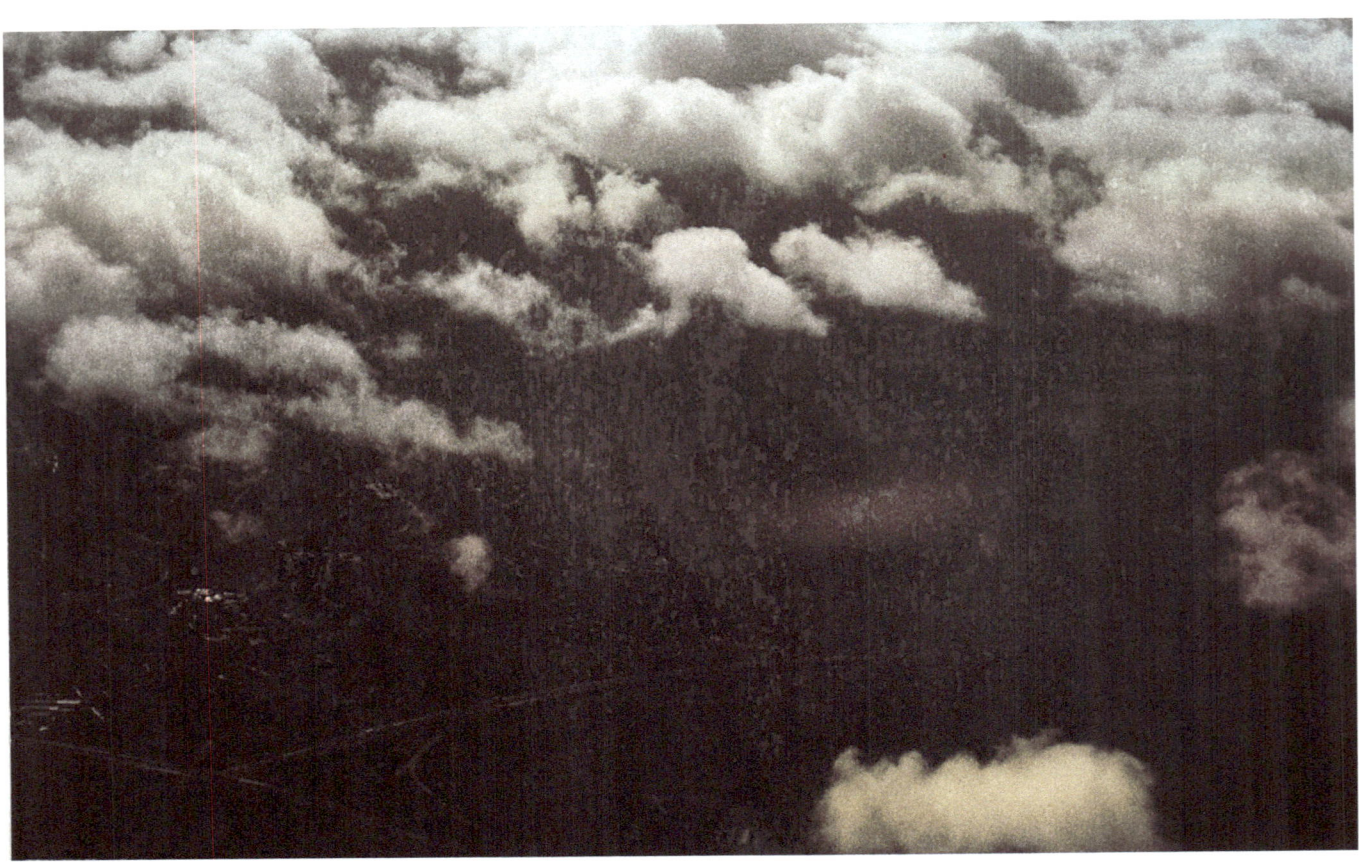

Leaving London Crop, *monoprint, 25 x 37*

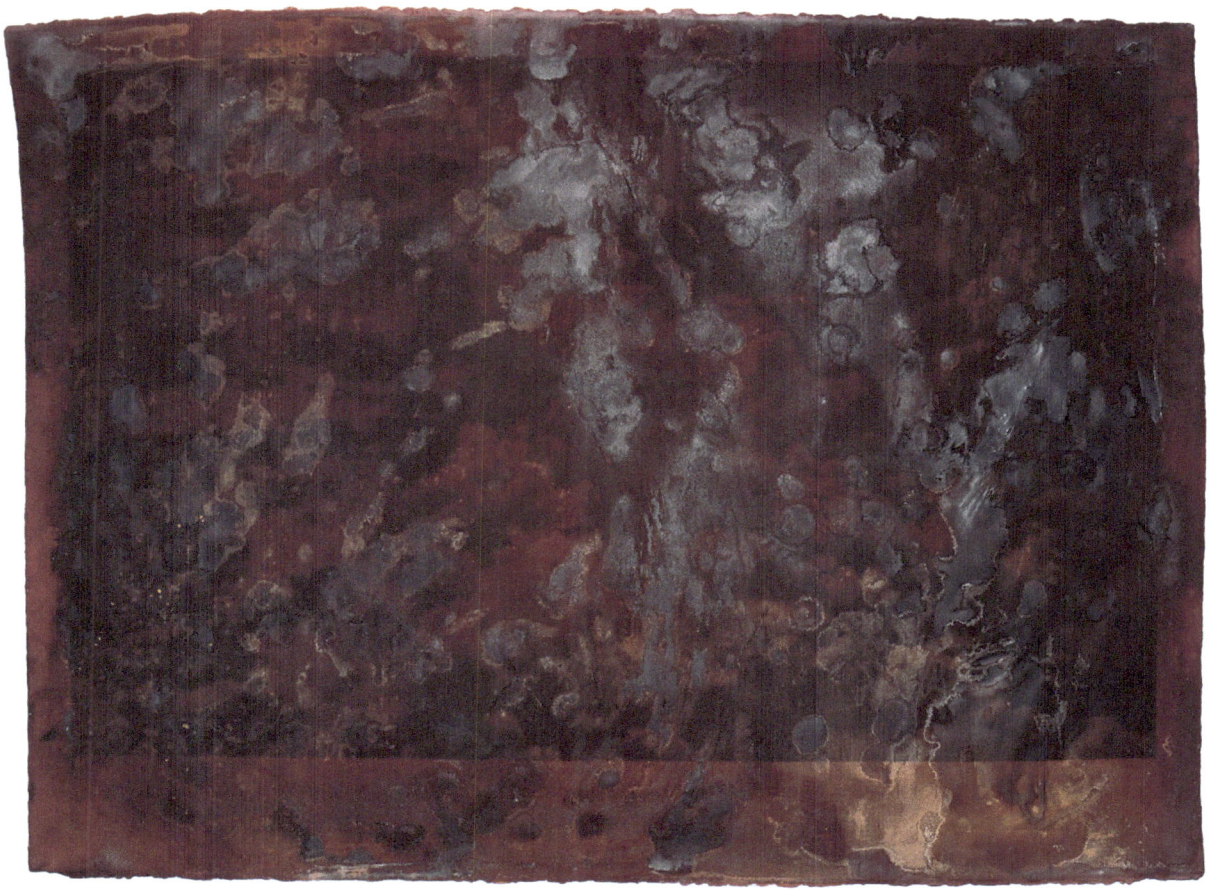

Night Falls, *monoprint, 25 x 33 inches*

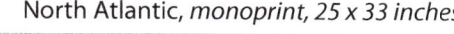

North Atlantic, *monoprint, 25 x 33 inches*

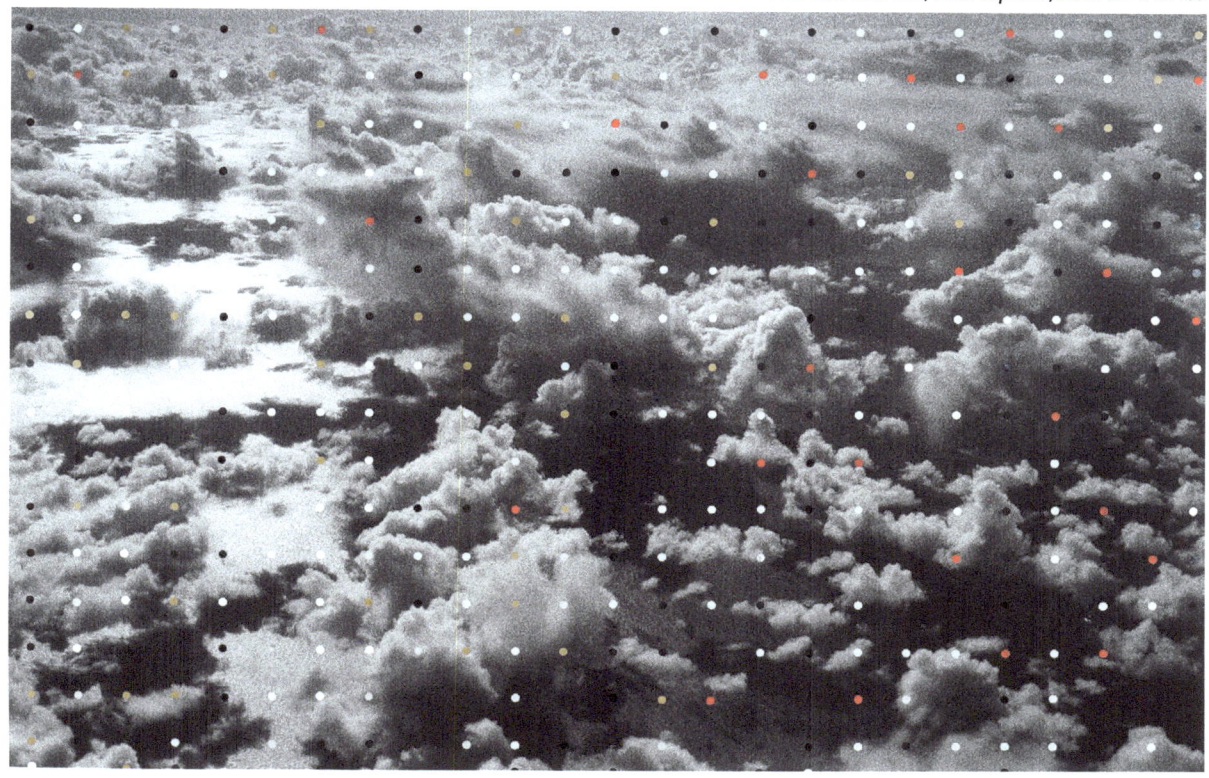

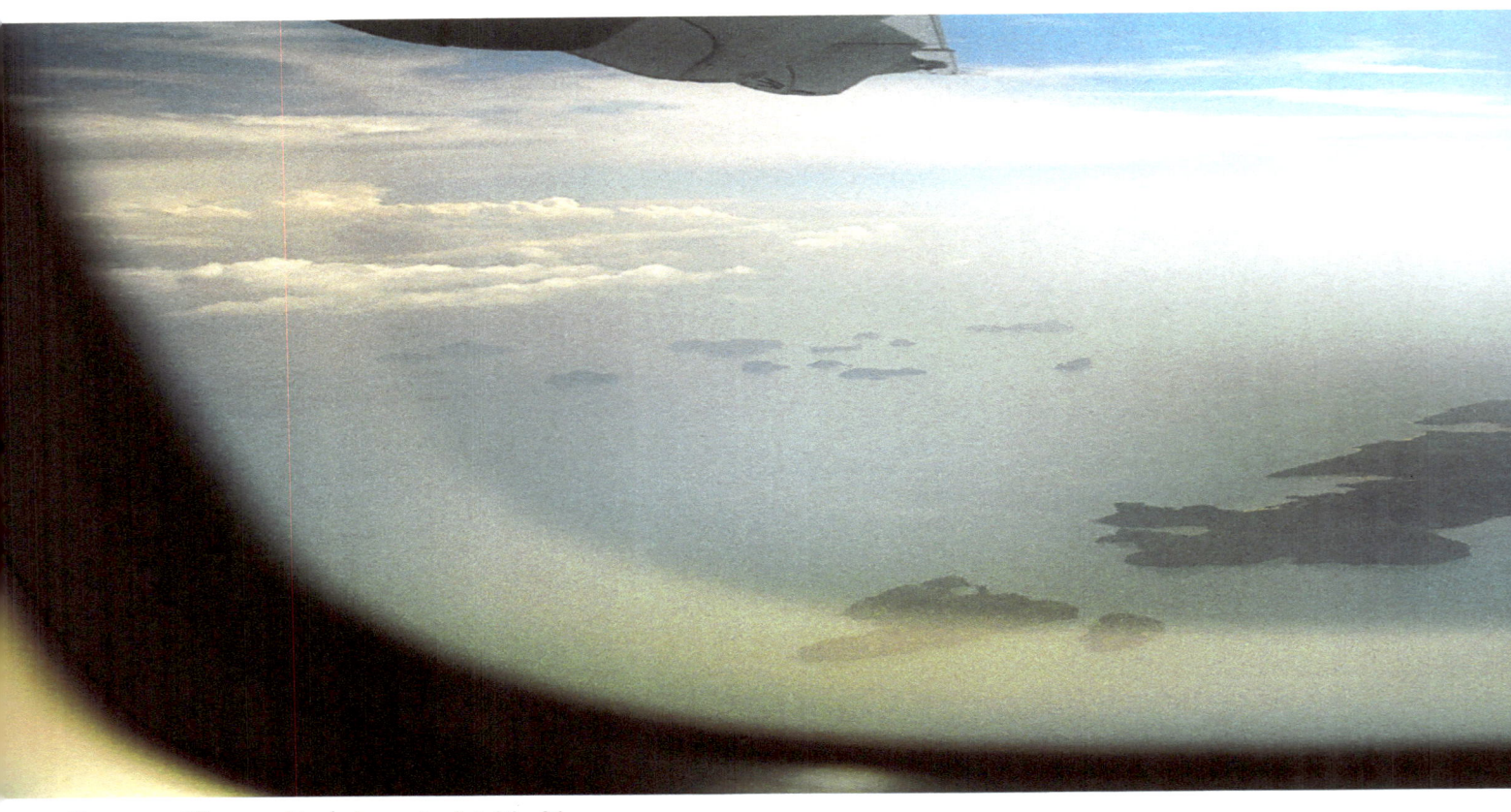

Singapore Sling, *archival pigment print, 36 x 96*

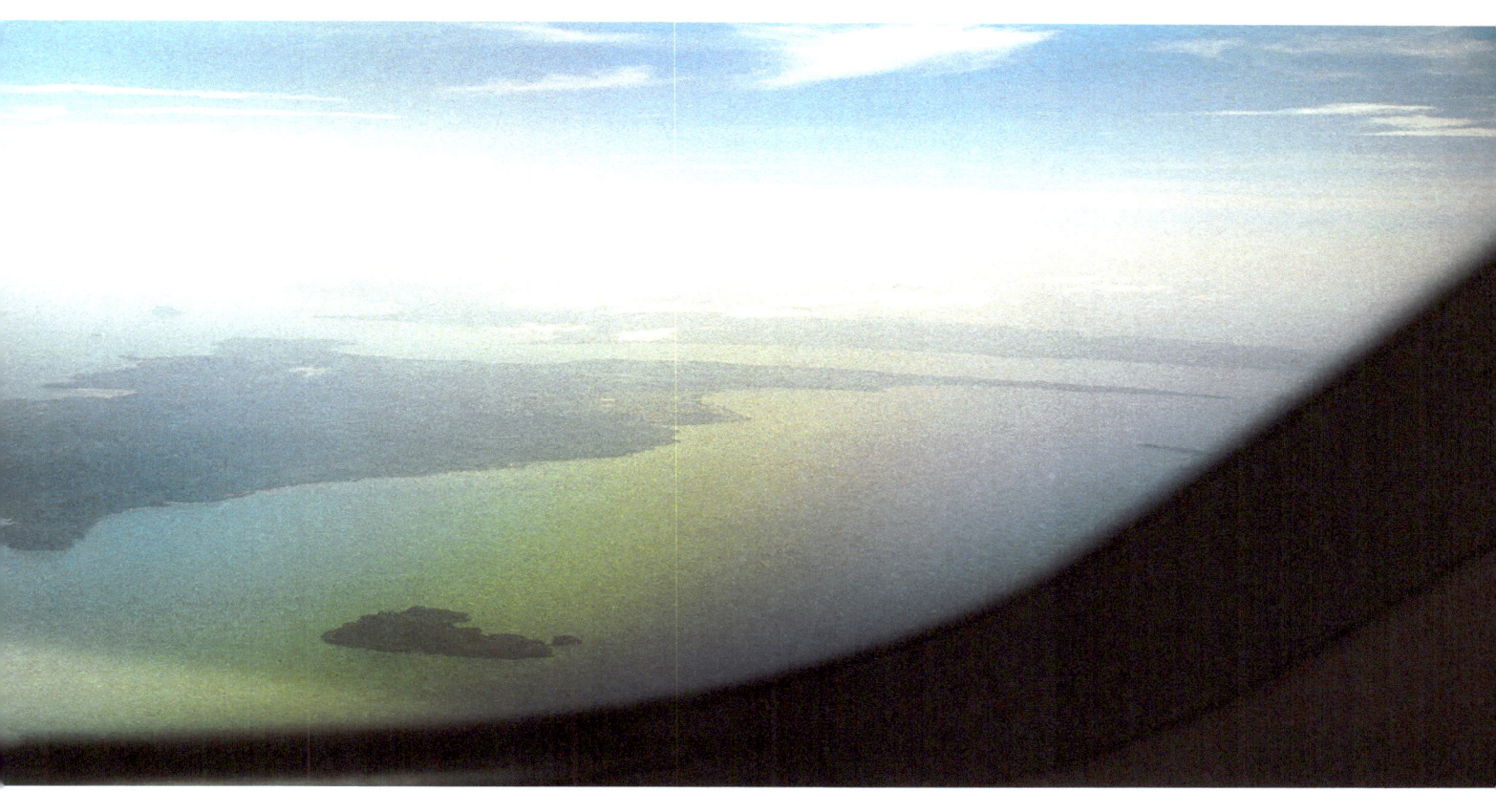

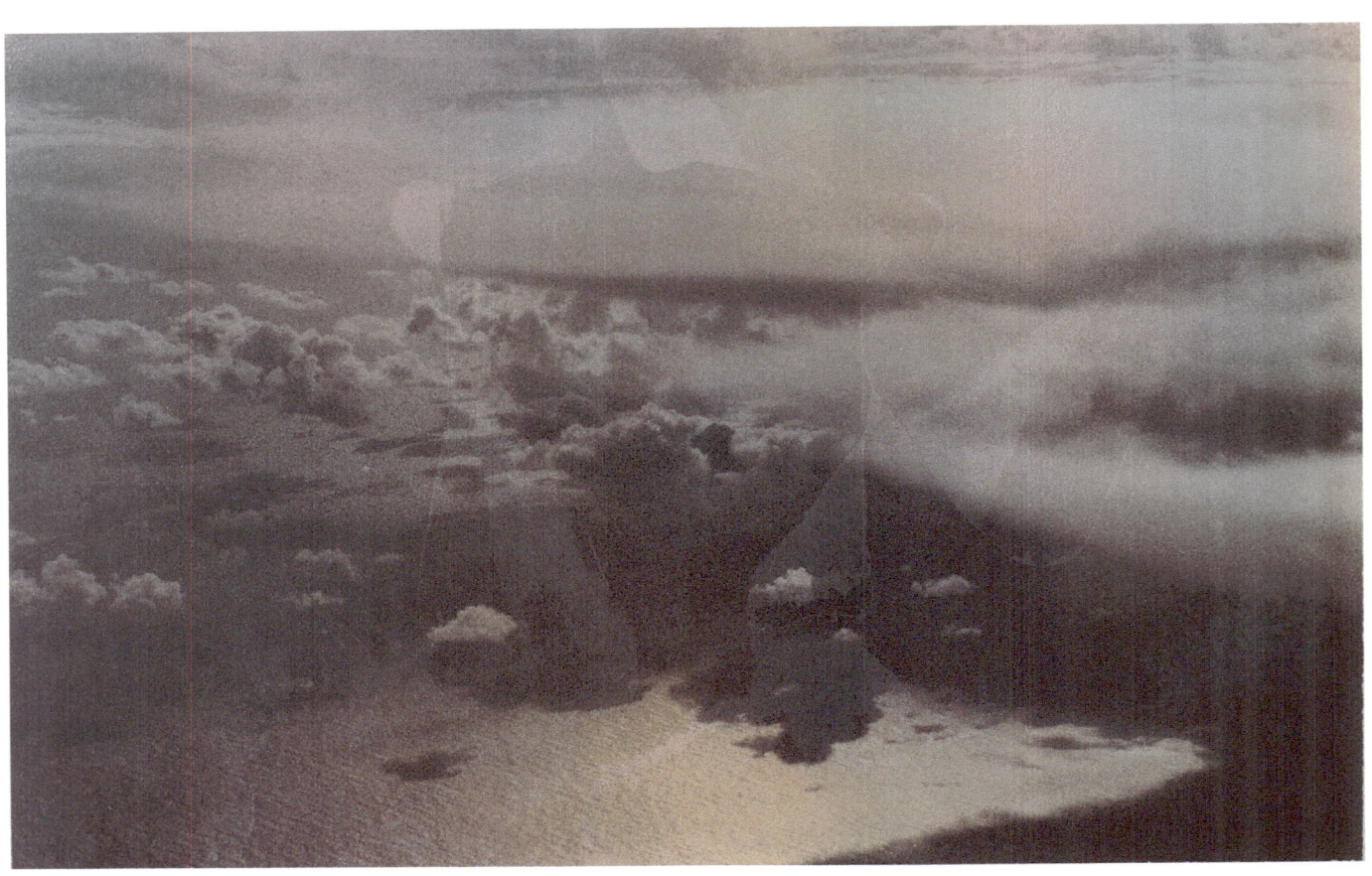

North Atlantic sunset, *monoprint, 25 x 37*

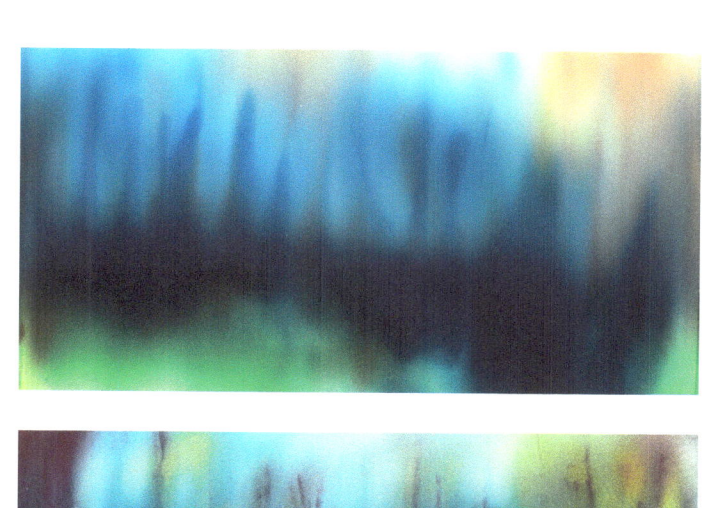

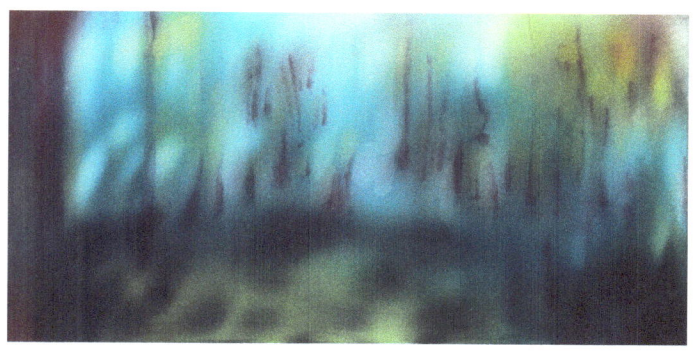

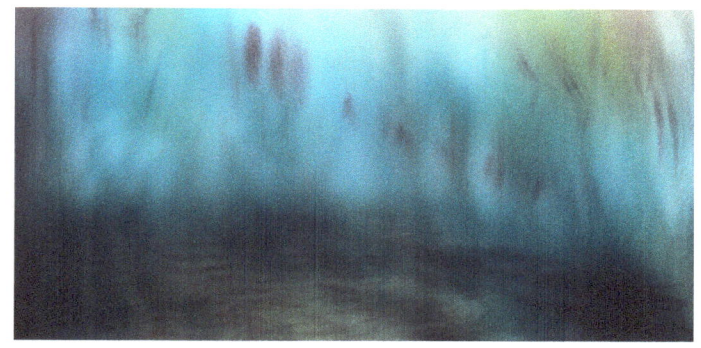

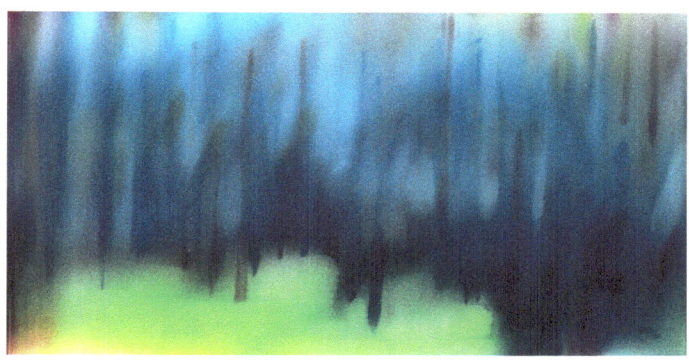

SCMist (series), *monotype, 18 x 35 inches each*

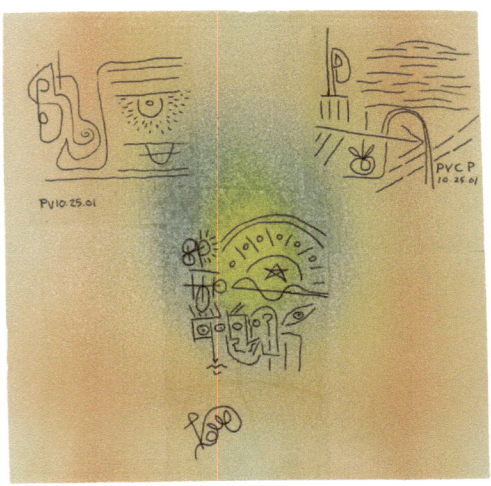
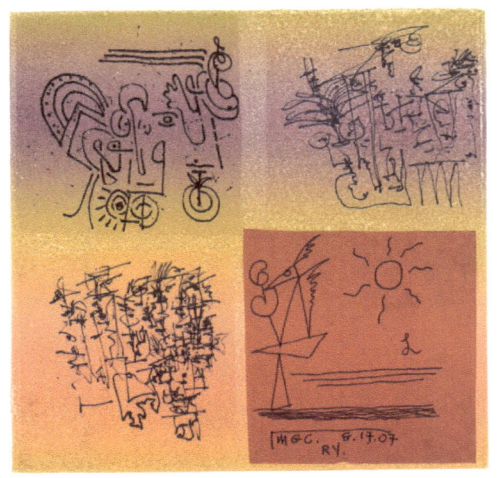
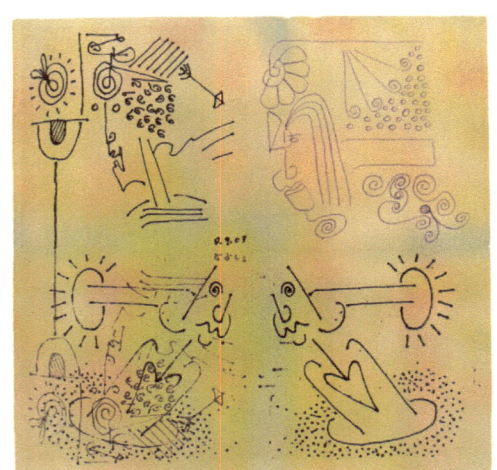
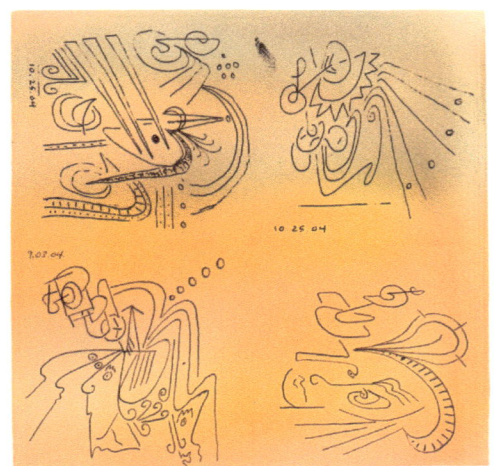
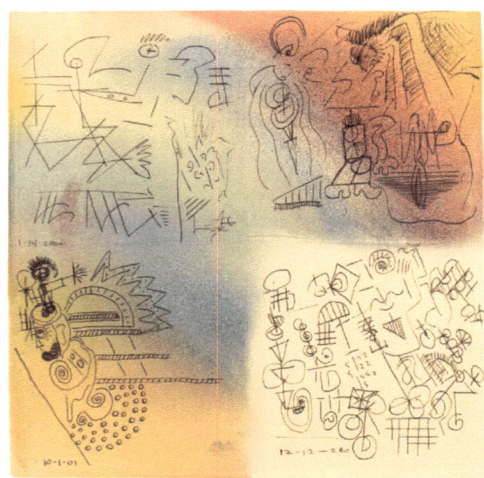
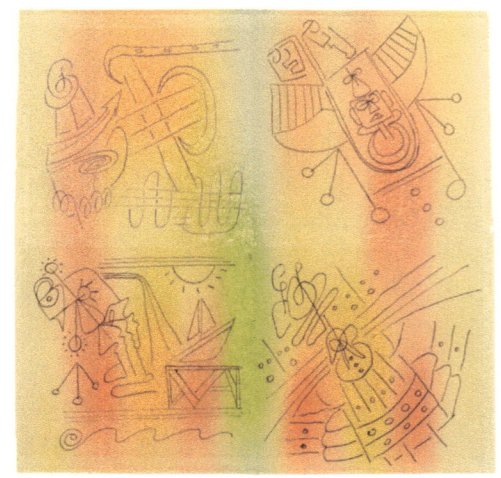

Untitled (Monotype Napkins), *chine collé monotype, 10 x 10 inches each*

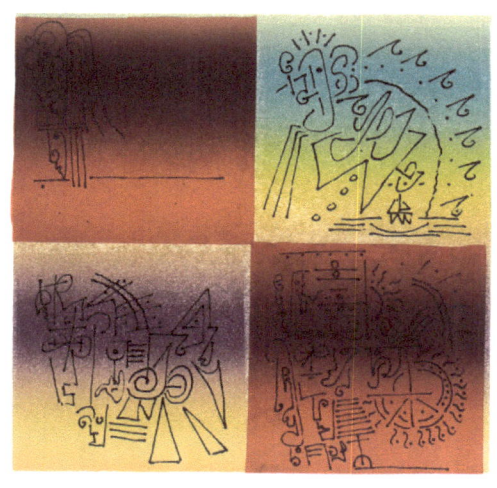
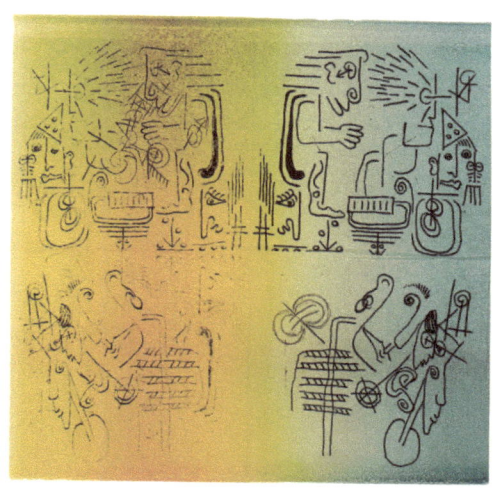
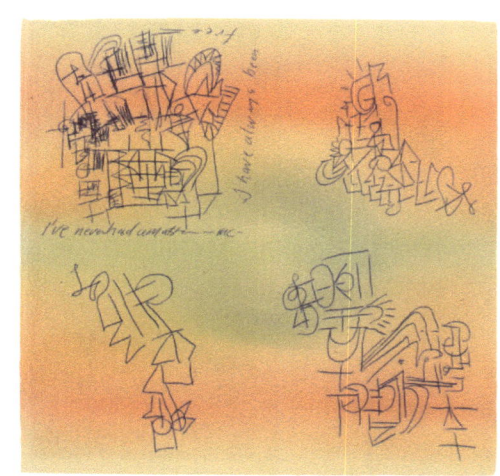
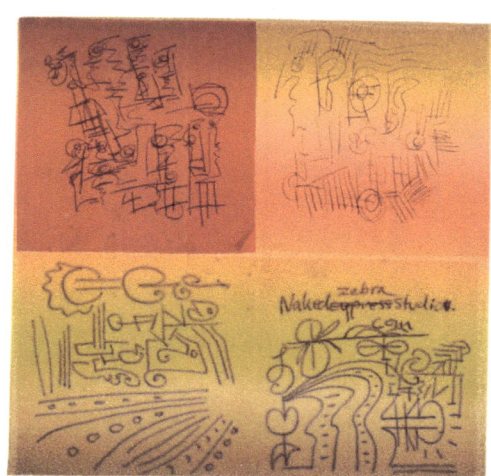
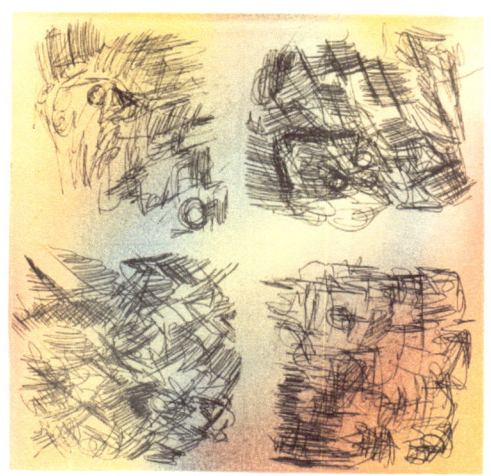
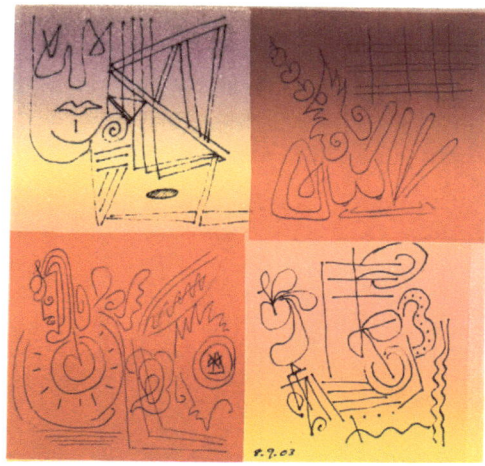

Untitled (Monotype Napkins), *chine collé monotype, 10 x 10 inches each*

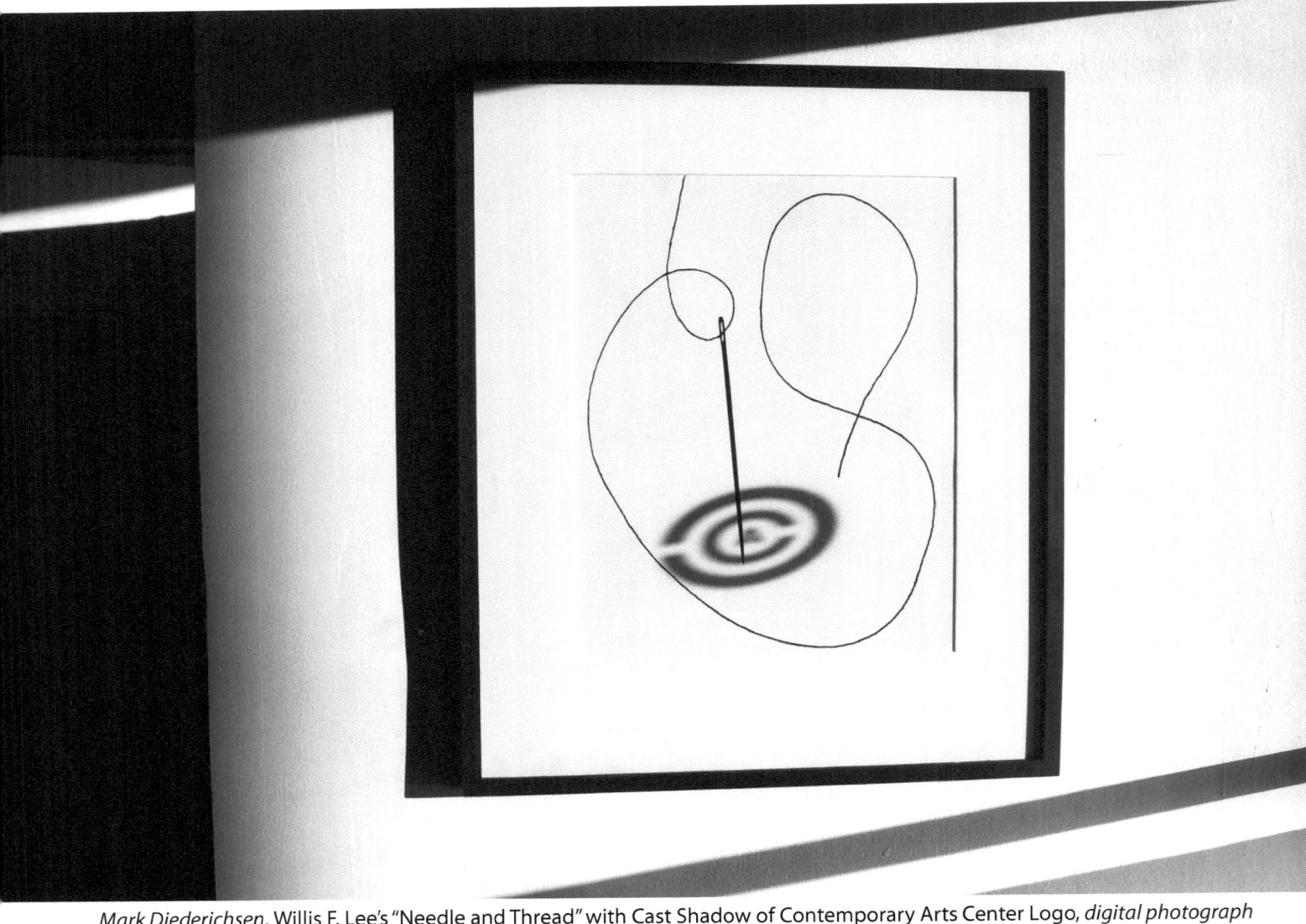

Mark Diederichsen, Willis F. Lee's "Needle and Thread" with Cast Shadow of Contemporary Arts Center Logo, *digital photograph*

www.ingramcontent.com/pod-product-compliance
Lightning Source LLC
Chambersburg PA
CBHW050806180526
45159CB00004B/1561